# CARL BARKS'
# DUCK

**Other Books In The Critical Cartoons Series:**

*Ed vs. Yummy Fur: Or, What Happens When a Serial Comic Becomes a Graphic Novel* by Brian Evenson

*Carl Barks' Duck: Average American*
Critical Cartoons 002

Copyright © 2014 Peter Schilling Jr. & Uncivilized Books.

All artwork is copyright © 2014 Disney Enterprises, Inc.

Series Editor/Art Director: Tom Kaczynski
Additional Design: Sean Ford
Copy Edits: Alec Berry
Production assistant: Rachel Topka

**Uncivilized Books**
P.O. Box 6434
Minneapolis, MN 55406
USA

uncivilizedbooks.com

First Edition, Dec 2014
10 9 8 7 6 5 4 3 2 1

ISBN 978-0-9889014-0-7

DISTRIBUTED TO THE TRADE BY:

**Consortium Book Sales & Distribution, LLC.**
34 Thirteenth Avenue NE,
Suite 101 Minneapolis,
MN 55413-1007
Orders: (800) 283-3572

Printed in Canada

CRITICAL CARTOONS

# CARL BARKS'
# DUCK

## AVERAGE AMERICAN

........................

**by Peter Schilling Jr.**

Uncivilized Books

*"Oh, he is so many types of characters..."*
—Carl Barks

# CONTENTS

Before I began to read comics, I indulged myself in "real" books. Books with words, maybe an illustration or two if it was a classic like *Huckleberry Finn*, but no comics whatsoever. As a nervous kid of the 1970s, I was content to retreat into novels, everything from *The Hobbit* to *Watership Down* to *The Red Pony*, and even an attempt at cracking *Moby-Dick* (at which I failed miserably, though that edition was illustrated.) As the product of divorced parents, whose mother allowed my brother and me one television show a week (but we could stay up an hour past bedtime with a book), and whose father didn't even have a television, I found myself lost in books over and over again, eager for new challenges (like Melville) but never the comics. They simply weren't my bag.

There were two reasons for this: first, we didn't have much money, and comic books cost money, even if they were only thirty-five cents at the time. My family found most of our reading material at the library, and libraries didn't have comics (many still don't, though that's improving.)

However, one day at the Bay City (Michigan) Central Library, a stately old brick building in the center of that ruined town, where I lost countless Saturday afternoons, I came across the *Smithsonian*

*Collection of Newspaper Comics*, that big, beautiful hardcover collection of old strips from long, lost newspapers, lovingly assembled by Bill Blackbeard and Martin Williams. God, that thing blew my mind with those brief glimpses of Segar's *Popeye*, Gottfredson's *Mickey Mouse*, and Walt Kelly's *Pogo* (among many others.) Granted, I did read the daily comic strips in the *Detroit Free Press*, like *Peanuts* and *Shoe* and *Tank McNamara*. But that was it for me, comic-wise, even though the Smithsonian collection made me want more.

The second problem, as I saw it, was that comic books were almost all about superheroes, and superheroes seemed to be the preferred reading material of assholes. Before readers of the Fantastic Four and the Dark Knight get all up in my grill, this was my experience as a child: I know a ton of good people now who adore superhero comics, and I myself read a bunch of the really great ones, *Plastic Man* and *The Spirit*, Jack Kirby's work, etc. At the time, however, I really loathed them and it was because the toughs and dickheads at my school all dug the superheroes. I know now that this was actually a fascinating time for Marvel and DC comics, their Silver Period, I guess, dealing with issues of that tumultuous decade, the inner-city violence, drug use and looking mod. Trying to fit in, I'd try one or two superhero comics borrowed from a some playground pal I didn't know all that well, but the stories seemed too macho for my tastes, and with way too much backstory and dumb violence. To a degree, I still think that's a problem today.

These are the mid- to late-70s I'm remembering, '75 to the dawning of the Reagan years. Now, as an adult, I love looking back at the crazy 70s, the bell bottom jeans, the amazing music and movies, the advertisements, virtually everything about that decade fascinates me. Look at the Green Lantern and Green Arrow comics of that time, with their funky outfits, their driving in a van across America, dealing with the ghetto and the drugs and the Man. That's really cool.

Back then, however, I was a sheepish, pale, timid boy who was almost literally scared of his own shadow. The 1970s tended to intimidate me, and though I went batty for 70s baseball and *Star Wars*, I tended to love old stuff more. Old books, old movies like *Citizen Kane* and *Singin' in the Rain* (yes, I watched *Kane* as a precocious ten-year-old, thanks to my Dad's prodding me that "there was more to life than *Star Wars*" and hauling us to the majestic Temple Theater in Saginaw to watch old movies), classical music and my parents' Beatles, Creedence, Fugs, and Stones albums, and the old Disney cartoons like *Pinocchio* and *Fantasia*. Kiss, *Grease, Welcome Back Kotter*, and all the classic 70s comics either eluded me or, quite honestly, frightened me.

Now my father grew up in the 1950s, and despite his being a leftist, an almost-hippie with his long hair and earring (radical in the 70s), growing pot in his bedroom closet, celebrating his vegetarian diet, protesting nuclear power and other subversive pursuits, paradoxically he still had a great affection for Walt Disney comics. As a child, he, like literally millions of others, subscribed to *Walt Disney's Comics and Stories*, and fell in love with Donald Duck and Uncle Scrooge stories especially. Every once in awhile he would pick up a Donald Duck comic from the local drugstore for my brother and me. This was a time when you didn't have to go to a comic book store to buy your swag—in fact, there weren't all that many comic book stores around. There was always a metal rack full of comics, Marvel and DC, Richie Rich and Disney Comics from Whitman publishing in virtually every pharmacy, K-mart, bookstore, and convenience store. Any place that sold magazines, really.

Problem was, most of the Disney material back then was pretty insulting to a kid's intelligence. God, I hated the Disney storytelling style, *The Apple Dumpling Gang, Escape to Witch Mountain*, and other crap with their silly villains who could be easily defeated by anyone with half a brain and an overripe banana as a weapon. (This was one of the many reasons I adored *Star Wars* and especially the badass Darth Vader.) For me, I wanted a good, solid story, with good, solid heroes and tough, solid villains. I wanted a decent adventure even if there were no villains.

And I got them, every once in awhile, from the Donald Duck comics that my Dad brought home. Sometimes, you'd get a Duck comic that was insipid. Other times, though, you got one that wasn't just fun, it was spectacular—witty, exciting, hilarious.

Problem was, neither my father nor myself nor my brother knew exactly how to find those "good" comics. These were, of course, the Donald Duck stories written and drawn by Carl Barks. Despite there existing a parallel universe in the 1970s where Carl Barks was being discovered and celebrated by rabid fans, young men who wrote letters to Disney and physically flew themselves to Southern California to meet the man, for the casual reader such as myself, I had no clue as to who wrote and drew these things. Obviously there wasn't an internet, and the revelation that Barks was one of the century's greatest comic book creators was the stuff of fanzines and journals that I didn't have access to, in small part because I didn't care at that age. Instead, I had to make due with the silly Duck stories as drawn by who-the-hell-knows, with their stumpy beaks and cheap backgrounds (not to mention terrible jokes and idiotic stories) or that guy whose lettering was architect-neat and whose ducks were drawn perfectly, his imaginative stories thrilling to the extreme.

In a sense, this was like walking up to a movie theater with a marquee that read "Warner Brothers" and one day you get *Battlefield Earth* another day you get *Jonah Hex* and on yet another day you get Howard Hawks' *The Big Slee*" or Terrence Malick's *Badlands*. You would be stunned by the latter two, hungry for more, hungry to find out just who made these beauties… except that the credits read that the director and writer—hell, everyone who worked on the film—is "The Warner Brothers." It was damned frustrating.

Then one day, in 1978, fortified with a bunch of birthday money, I made my way to the local bookstore. There, at the exorbitant price of

$25, was a white coffee-table tome simply titled "Donald Duck", with a large picture of Donald, tongue out in determination, chasing after an hourglass. Walt's manufactured signature was up top, and there was a little gold and blue ribbon stamped in the upper-right hand corner that read "Best Comics". No slip cover, just pure white on the back. This was a strange publishing venture (even by today's high standards) from some concern called Abbeville Press out of New York City.

I sat down and began to read, though I didn't get far. Thumbing through the book, I instantly recognized that they were all the "good" Donald Duck stories that I'd come to love. Then I glanced at the introduction, and read:

> *Being the author and illustrator of the ten short novels*
> *that appear on the following pages...*

There he was: Carl Barks. I immediately bought the book, using up all my birthday money and a bit more savings, and raced home to read these little masterpieces. That thing really turned me on to what remains my favorite comic book character, Donald Duck, and it was a perfect introduction to Barks, even if in this edition the coloring is a bit bright and they reformatted each to fit onto such tall pages. Barks, in his introduction, states that the material is "not juvenile kids' stuff," which made me feel all grown-up, and the stories themselves were amazing. From "Frozen Gold," with Donald going snowblind in the tundra as he tries to deliver penicillin to poor Alaskans; to "Lost in the Andes," perhaps Barks' most highly regarded story (the one with the square eggs); to one of my two personal favorites, then and now, "The Golden Helmet," featuring a race for the eponymous treasure that would essentially give its owner tyrannical control over North America and all its people. From then on, I was hooked, and tried to find Barks' stories whenever and wherever I could.

Since then, I've read probably everything by the "Duck Man", from his Donald Duck tales to his hugely popular Uncle Scrooge stories. I've spent way too much money on an almost complete set of wonderful Bruce Hamilton Company versions under the Gladstone Publishing imprint, *The Carl Barks Library of Donald Duck Adventures*, *Walt Disney's Comics and Stories*, and *Uncle Scrooge Adventures*, all of which have intense essays by devoted followers of Barks. And I will continue to buy the new and absolutely perfect Fantagraphics editions, which is really the way to go nowadays, both economically and in terms of layout.

A few people have asked me why I'm focusing on Donald Duck, as opposed to the Uncle Scrooge comics, which seem to excite people a lot more. There are a number of favorite Uncle Scrooge comics of mine, especially "Land Beneath the Ground," featuring the Terry Fermians, the creatures who make earthquakes; and Scrooge's battle against Flintheart Glomgold in "Second-Richest Duck," among others (and isn't Flintheart Glomgold the coolest name ever?). But to me Uncle Scrooge is a single-minded character and the stories involve a single-minded pursuit, namely, that of protecting Scrooge's vast wealth—not making more wealth (which, in itself, might actually be interesting considering the variety of ways one might generate income.) Now, Barks did a lot within that narrow focus, but I find that reading Scrooge comics at length eventually becomes tiresome, Donald and the boys reduced to grumbling factotums who never get their proper pay and are usually tricked into doing the work in the first place. Ultimately, in the end, Scrooge either beats the Beagle Boys (who are, to a dog, fairly rote characters) or Magica De Spell (yet another mediocre female in the Barks universe), learns some lesson about being kind to people (or not), and keeps his money bin intact. For the most part, Scrooge always wins. And sometimes they end with Scrooge happily swimming in his money, a conclusion that profoundly depressed me as a child, just as it does now.

On the other hand, Donald Duck is an actor, like a favorite star from

Hollywood's Golden Age. I know of no other comic book or comic strip character who functions in quite the same way. Yes, he's always Donald Duck, but following him is the same as enjoying the work of Cary Grant, Jimmy Stewart or Buster Keaton, actors whose movies I think are similar to the Donald Duck stories in the Barks oeuvre. Like Grant or Stewart—name your favorites from Hollywood's Studio System years—Donald wears dozens of figurative hats, while essentially remaining himself, in the same way that Cary Grant is Cary Grant even if he's a newspaper editor, a scientist, or a pilot. We marvel when Donald slips into a new role, eagerly anticipating the approaching storm when he becomes… well, the list is as amazing as it is almost endless: Donald Duck has been a barber, a lumberjack, lifeguard, restaurateur, short order cook, salesman of various products (from brushes to steam calliopes), museum guard, night watchman, gardener, Olympic athlete, egg farmer, photographer, tightrope walker, fishing guide, chemist, falconer, rainmaker, bill collector, fireman, cowboy… literally dozens of different jobs, and he approaches each one with varying degrees of skill or none at all.

What other comic book (or comic strip) character plays so many different roles? You tell me—far as I know, the superheroes were consistently the same, Richie Rich, Krazy Kat, Pogo, Tintin, even Uncle Scrooge (and the rest of Barks' characters) and everyone in the comics universe have their lives and do pretty much the same thing with them, with story lines revolving around who and what they are and what they have been up to. Donald Duck, on the other hand, has no continuity between his stories, outside of the fact that he has these three nephews and he lives in either Burbank or Duckburg. He has character—a bad temper, an inability to listen most of the time, an eagerness to jump headlong into an adventure—but in one story he's a master at a certain profession, in another a total failure, a farmer one day, a guard the next, fill in the blank.

Despite Barks' calling his stories "novels," or "theater" as he does in a 1994 interview for Danish television, I think of these stories in the way I think of movies, essentially "paper movies," the panels composed similarly, the "editing"—the leaving out of superfluous visual information to heighten what we do see—has a timing like the best movies. Barks' paper movies have a star, and his name is Donald Duck.

Part of great comedy involves anticipation, and expecting the worst from an obvious situation can be damned funny. When we hear that Cary Grant is a scientist or Laurel and Hardy are hired to move a piano, we can't wait to see what happens. There's actually not a lot in the classic Laurel and Hardy short "The Music Box" that is a genuine surprise (that's the one where they haul a player piano up about ten billion steps), but it is the unfolding disaster that excites us. So it is with Donald Duck. When we hear that he's Duckburg's greatest glass maker, as he is in 1959's "The Master Glasser", the mind reels at the spectacle of broken glass and wreckage that we know is coming. We can smell the story baking, and gorge ourselves on that glorious loaf of chaos. Donald Duck is a character in a series of great adventures and outright comedies that seem to rival the best work that came out of the Hollywood studio system, which I think the Disney combine resembles (albeit without any of the artist recognition that, say, Howard Hawks and others enjoyed.)

Barks created such a believable character probably because he himself related most to Donald. "I was a fizzle as a cowboy, a logger, a printing press feeder, a steelworker, a carpenter, an animator, a chicken grower, and a barfly," Barks admitted. His experience with chickens certainly plays a part in the stories—Donald fails at raising chickens or is involved with chickens in numerous stories, from a wonderful little story called "Omelet" to "Lost in the Andes" and even in "The Magic Hourglass", where an egg sets the story in motion. I'm not going to go too much into Barks' life, except to say that this background, this series of failures, informs his work, just as Barks' endless inability to make a lot of money resulted, sadly for him but happily for us, in his fixating on writing and drawing these great comics.

Carl Barks labored under this system, blessed with a third wife who appreciated his work, blessed with the humility to work without recognition for two decades for Disney (and Western Publishing directly), blessed to have such little interest in travel and luxury living that allowed him to direct all of his considerable energies into the Duck stories and not get upset that he never had any money to go out and live a little. Barks essentially made a decent living, probably not a whole lot more than your average schoolteacher (probably less in some years), failed at just about every money-making scheme he concocted, and eventually drifted into retirement and a belated recognition from his fans. In this retirement, he made oil paintings of the ducks that have none of the charm of his early work, but brought in some well needed dough, and made his fan base happy. Sad in a way, and maybe a bit Willy Loman, but that's what happened.

Donald Duck shares some of these traits, even as he is wildly different. Here I am going to take a somewhat contradictory position from many Barks' critics and even Barks himself. Critic Thomas Andrae said of Donald, "No one tried harder—or failed more miserably—to attain the American dream," and Barks himself stated many times that his creation is "unlucky." I find this somewhat true but essentially off-the-mark: Donald fails constantly, to our pleasure, but he succeeds more often that you'd think. Donald does not typically succeed financially. But he does emerge from many of these stories with his dignity intact and with a spiritual success in the face of economic ruin that is unmatched (though sometimes, as you'll see, he does simply emerge rich, though it is a wealth that never follows him into another story.) Like Donald, most of us fail, which is why he is so approachable. But Donald's mounting losses never seem oppressive to us because he's actually won a few times, but even in the worst of his defeats, when the final panels show him bent over from his failure, or wrecking a place because his frustrations have finally mounted, Donald always keeps us dreaming, because you know what? His life is still amazing.

The best cinematic analogy I can think of is Steven Spielberg's *Raiders of the Lost Ark*. Would you call that a movie about failure? No, you wouldn't. And yet Indiana Jones gets the Ark, but we don't see him benefit financially by the prize, nor professionally—in fact, in that famous final shot, we see that his treasure is taken and lost in a warehouse representing a vast, Kafkaesque bureaucracy. But who among us doesn't think of his journey as a great success?

Donald seeks adventure because this is what makes life worth living. In many of his stories you will find a character who embarks on a journey—to save North America for instance—for nothing other than the fact that he can. Donald never seems to blink an eye dropping everything to seek his fortune, even if that fortune is only spiritual.

This little book is not—I repeat, NOT—an exhaustive study of Carl Barks' work. First of all, there's a few of those out there, from Thomas Andrae's *Carl Barks and the Disney Comic Book* to the essays in all the Hamilton books, to the lovingly curated Carl Barks' site, www. CBarks.dk, run by the friendly Peter Kylling, to the somewhat famous (or infamous, depending on who you talk to) Marxist critique, *How to Read Donald Duck* by Ariel Dorfman and Armand Mattelart (subtitled *Imperialist Ideology in the Disney Comic*—this was originally published in Chile and banned in the U.S. for a time!) All of these will give you everything you need to know about the man and his work, even, on CarlBarks.dk, how much he was paid to create each story, which I find fascinating.

No, this is an appreciation, my attempt at convincing you, a casual comic book reader, to put this book down eventually and head over and read some of Barks' work. Here you will find seven separate essays on my nine favorite Donald Duck "novels" and the best of his "work" stories, shorter pieces wherein Donald is somehow a master of a certain craft—he is the best there is at, say, rainmaking, but then he runs afoul of his own ego and essentially destroys his business, or Duckburg, or both.

The stories chosen are my own personal favorites, though I did break from my top ten and included other favorites (farther down the list) that give you a glimpse of Donald interacting with prominent characters in the Barks' universe, such as Uncle Scrooge and Gladstone Gander, or certain stories that are quintessential Donald. So, for instance, I've included "The Magic Hourglass," which is one of my favorites, but it beat out, say, "Frozen Gold," because it will be the one story I chose to cover that involves Uncle Scrooge, albeit a wicked, greedy Scrooge, and one that evokes not only Frank Norris' *McTeague* but also Erich von Stroheim's film version *Greed* (but more on that later.)

Sadly, it'll take some time, and some money, for you to indulge in many of these suggestions, should you desire such a treat, as Fantagraphics is still releasing the Carl Barks stories, roughly two volumes a year (albeit chock full of stories.) You can go online and get many of the Gladstone editions, but they'll set you back a pretty penny. For now, I encourage you to seek these out however you can, with whatever resources are at your disposal.

So set aside your preconceptions about all things Disney, and marvel at these incredible adventures and comedies. For I'm serious when I say that Carl Barks' Donald Duck stories are brilliant "paper movies," an American pop culture phenomenon to rank up there with screwball comedies of the 30s and the best adventure serials. If I do my job right, you'll be hiding your Donald Duck book behind your *Wall Street Journal* on the bus or subway, or shouting at your kids to let you have "Lost in the Andes" back.

Fig. 1. Maharajah Donald, 2:2

# THE PENCIL STUB THAT LAUNCHED A SHIP:
## *Maharajah Donald*

Look at the splash panel at the top of "Maharajah Donald:" There's Donald, sitting ramrod straight on a luxurious pile of presumably silken pillows, turbaned, holding a golden scepter, his head up and eyes closed to his sweating nephews who stare up at him in either wonder or worry. How did this loafing, unsuccessful citizen of Burbank, California end up here? And why are his nephews so worried?

Back in the 1970s, and I imagine back in the 1940s (when this story was first released to children at department stores), it was the height of adventure to send a favorite character off to exotic lands, to have magazine pictorials, perhaps to give the folks at home a sense of how beautiful it was in the countries where dad fought in the good war. *National Geographic, Life*, the Hope and Crosby[1] films—these took us untraveled Americans around the world, and made them feel accessible, safe, even if they were totally patronizing, usually racist (always?), and sanitized for our protection. This didn't change much

....................
1    The Hope & Crosby "Road to…" films were ridiculous, though enormously popular, travel movies, wherein Bing Crosby (the straight man who gets the girl) and Bob Hope (the eye-rolling jokester) travel to foreign lands and make all sorts of funny. Americans loved them for their exotic locales. They are unbelievably bad and not worth watching today.

by the 1970s, except that a lot of countries were beginning to assert themselves against America's intellectual and military attitude of superiority.

However, even if you welcomed this chaos—as my Dad, a man who cut his teeth protesting in the 60s and 70s, did—stories like "Maharajah Donald," with their old school attitude, nonetheless have that grand air of adventure; a Joseph Campbell sense of heroes revealing themselves through sheer chance. And, they are entertaining as all hell. This is early Barks, a story where we see him, and maybe even his hero, cutting their teeth, wriggling into their roles and trying to make them fit.

From that splash panel giving us a clue of Donald's strange fate, we cut to our "hero," such as he is, standing in front of his garage, beckoning the same nephews to come and haul away the accumulated junk that threatens to tumble out into the street. He makes a deal: "When you're finished, I'll give you any of the junk I don't want to keep!"[2] But the next panel sees a close-up of Donald, smiling, saying to himself, "They work real hard when they think they're going to get paid!"

From there the story takes off. "Maharajah Donald" is the first of the early Donald Duck comics (it was Barks' seventh full-length story) that I think is worthy of extensive commentary. In the first page, from that first panel, we're already sent rolling into what we know will turn out to be a crazy story. This is one of the few, if only, stories where the splash panel gives us a mysterious clue as to the climax of the story—usually the panel serves as a bold beginning as opposed to foreshadowing. Donald will somehow become a Maharajah, but then Barks drags us back home, and this adventure begins in a garage, in the stifling banality of Burbank (where Barks' early Duck stories were

...................

2  Barks always ends his sentences with an exclamation point and often bolds specific words for effect—with every quote from a comic that I use, the emphasis is always Barks'.

situated.) The nephews, good and earnest, will get screwed by their jerk of an uncle and, probably, save the day with their wit and pluck. And this happens. Watching it unfold is the fun, and the method by which the kids launch this adventure makes the reader believe that this could happen to them. Implausible, perhaps, but stranger things have happened.

At the time of "Maharajah Donald," Barks was writing numerous stories in which Donald would lord over the only people who could be lorded over by such a shiftless loaf—namely, his nephews, Huey, Dewey and Louie. Naturally, they rebel—this was in fact a variation on the theme of the nephews being Katzenjammer-like[3] kids in the cartoons, but expanded and made richer in the comics. Here, as in many other stories, the nephews are mischievous but also hardworking, intelligent, and capable of very adult behavior, in fact, more adult than their guardian. They do not do mischief simply for the sake of discord, waiting to be suppressed by punitive adults. No, the nephews react to the very improper and mean-spirited (not to mention cowardly) behavior on the part of their uncle. Admittedly, I am not a huge fan of this plotline, and the better stories (as you will see) involve a nice balance between all the ducks sniping at one another but eventually helping each other out. Here, the nephews do all the saving.

This young trio was named after Huey Long, Thomas Dewey (ambitious governors of Louisiana and New York, respectively), and Louis Schmitt, an animator at Disney, for whatever that's worth. They are the perfect foil to Donald, and if you're a kid, they're a nice way to connect to each story. I'm not entirely sure young characters are necessary for children to appreciate any story, much less a Donald

........................

3 *The Katzenjammer Kids* was one of the earliest and most popular newspaper strips (the first to use word balloons), written by Rudolph Dirks and drawn by Harold H. Knerr. The stories were essentially always the same—two brothers, younger boys, who wreak havoc on the world. Such was their popularity that they became synonymous with unruly children.

Fig. 2. Maharajah Donald, 2:3

Duck tale, but they do serve to leaven Donald's lunacy and pettiness, and at times force him to confront his own responsibilities.[4]

The next two pages reveal these kids to be remarkably resourceful and optimistic. After sweating out a whole afternoon cleaning out the garage, Donald inspects what is left over, and keeps nearly everything—an old radio, sleeping bag, a telescope, even old socks—until finally settling on giving the boys a pencil stub. In one brilliant panel, we see all three kids with different expressions, and saying very different things. (see Fig. 2)

A caveat and a digression: I don't own an original of *March of Comics* #4, where "Maharajah Donald" originally appeared. First of all, my mind reels at the way these stories were disseminated. The *March of Comics* was an idea of Western Publishing. It was a smaller-sized comic book that was distributed, literally in the millions, to stores around the United States that did brisk business to children. The vendor, say Sears, would have their name and logo on the front,

. . . . . . . . . . . . . . . . . . . .

4   Please note, I will refer to the ducks in human terms throughout this book, as they're essentially people.

and the kids could get the free book, presumably with a sale (maybe not), and have something to pore over while (again presumably) Mom would drag the kids around shopping.

This issue's cover featured Donald dressed, inexplicably, as Napoleon, his hand in his coat, giant hat atop his head, with Mickey Mouse snapping his photograph while one of the kids sits atop the camera, looking into the lens. This cover was not drawn by Barks, but what makes this promotion so intriguing to me is, again, the way in which this art was distributed. Here we have this great story, in a free comic book, Barks' name and identity completely hidden, given away to literally millions of children and then, poof, ten years later (or less) they're gone, for the most part. Millions of copies, tossed away. Now they're worth decent coin.

I'm also bringing this up because I have no idea as to the actual color of the boys' hats, which was later used to distinguish who they were, to a limited degree. What that means is that I also don't really know who is who, and neither does anyone else, including Barks. The two editions of "Maharajah Donald" that I do have—the Abbeville Press book mentioned in the introduction and Volume 6 of Gladstone Publishing's *The Carl Barks Library of Donald Duck Adventures in Color*—are colored digitally. The three nephews are meant, according to Barks, to be interchangeable, to be one unit, one organism, really. Barks drew in black and white, so he didn't care how Western colored their hats, didn't care to distinguish them at all. In fact, the nephews' hats, which became red, blue and green, were originally red, yellow and green, the yellow eventually giving way to blue.

So there is absolutely no way to tell the difference between the three, here and in the other comics, so I'm going to go by The Disney Corporation's later explanation, when the Ducktales series of television cartoons came out, that Dewey wears a blue hat, Huey wears a red hat, and Louie wears a green one. In the interest of a clearer narrative, this will help to explain just who's talking in any given panel, even as

Fig. 3. Maharajah Donald, 2:4

Barks' doesn't really care if we know who's speaking.

But back to the story. Given the pencil stub, and woefully underpaid for their labors, Dewey grumbles about their Uncle's largess, Louie makes a sarcastically happy face and says "So generous!", while Huey makes a rather wicked face and says "Don't rob yourself Unca' Donald." Despite being screwed, they seem defiant and determined. In fact, in the very next panel, the wheels are already beginning to turn.

In a nice visual break from the preceding panels, (see Fig. 3) Barks shows his three little protagonists in silhouette, and already they're working an angle. "Let's see what we can trade for it!" one says, and of course we have no idea who is speaking because, in shadow, we can't see their hat colors (and perhaps this speaks to Barks' total lack of interest in identifying each duckling.) But it doesn't matter, for the kids are about to go on a trading spree.

This spree, short though it is, encompassing fourteen panels and just over two pages. Pencil stub is swapped for a ball of string, string for a jackknife (to a poor kid whose kite has run out of string—the boys admit to highway robbery), knife for a silver belt buckle, and then, "some hours later" a camera for a "genuine poil me pop sent me from de south seas!" Unsure as to whether this pearl, which looks to be about the size of a superball, is real or paste, the trio hauls it to a jeweler, and there they meet some high-hat who gawks in amazement. This gentleman, clad in a top hat, spats, bow tie, and pinstriped pants, needs that pearl, as "it's exactly the size to complete my wife's necklace" (in what remains one of the very few moments where an actual married relationship is mentioned in a Disney comic book.)

In keeping with the spirit of the story thus far, Huey, Dewey and Louie turn down this man's offer to buy the pearl, asking instead for a trade ("whatcha got?"). And so Mr. Moneybags gives them the only thing other than money that he's willing to part with: a steamship ticket to India.

Barks was a tourist of his own imagination, relying heavily on his beloved collection of *National Geographic* (which he subscribed to the whole of his life and, like so many other subscribers, kept proudly displayed on bookshelves) to give him ideas. Unable to afford travel of any kind, and someone who did not see the world through the military (in fact, Barks was a strange combination of right-wing conservative and anti-war isolationist who thought World War II was a mistake), he roamed the world vicariously through the comics he drew. In later interviews he admitted to disliking leaving home, though that may be a product of his age at the time. Perhaps this is what makes Barks' work so effective—the Ducks maneuverings through India (and other locales we will examine later) were really the only way he himself was ever going to see much of the world outside of Hemet, the California village where he spent his days. The more detail he could put in a comic book, the better, for both him and his readers.

The high seas and India provide "Maharajah Donald" with its most effective panels. In later works, Donald's city of residence (Burbank here, Duckburg later) becomes a vibrant city, its parks almost jungles, its streets rich with detail (cars, people, posters on the walls). Here, the city is relatively flat, as bereft of detail as a *Peanuts* strip. But look at India! Here we have vast forests, crowded cities, the outfits, tigers, elephants, the works.

Once the kids have their ticket to ride, Donald instantly (and correctly) surmises that the boys aren't going anywhere, not the least because this is passage for one. "I am going to India! Pack my bags, infants!" he says, pointing with disdain. So not only are the kids' labors in the garage paid for with less-than-peanuts, the fruit of their additional labors (in trading those less-than-peanuts) are stolen and the kids are ordered to do even more work. This time for nothing.

However, unlike their Uncle Donald, a loafer extraordinaire, the kids won't mope and complain—they scheme and ponder and get their adventure.

In a sense, "Maharajah Donald" is almost not a Donald Duck comic, and this is one of the reasons I'm including it here. This is the story of kids, kids who still take orders from their guardian, but who are the engines of the story; the masters of their fate. Without them, we don't get on a steamer for the far east. Without them, we don't end up in the fictional country of Bumpay. Without them, Donald doesn't become a maharajah, and without them he doesn't get almost eaten by tigers.

When they stow-away on the boat, and are then discovered, Donald claims not to know his nephews. Forced to work for their passage, the boys grumble while their uncle enjoys his trip. Upon docking in Calcutta, the trio steals Donald's passport in order to keep him from being able to disembark ("If we can't land in Calcutta, neither can you!") an action which then propels us into the next act, when an effete man in a turban and a western-style suit offers to "solve their problem" in "return for a –(cough)– small favor."

This gent is the Maharajah of Hoopadoola, who takes the Ducks deep into India, to his gold-domed palace, where they're clothed and fed and wondering just what it is this guy could possibly want. Though not one of his greatest splash panels, we can almost imagine the scene at the bottom of page 11 in Cinemascope, our heroes gaping at the Taj Mahal-like palace in wonder. (see Plate 1)

Well, the favor, when it arrives, is a doozy: the Maharajah of Hoopadoola asks them to ride an old elephant across the river to the neighboring Kingdom of Bumpay... at gunpoint. See, whomever crosses the river becomes the Maharajah of Bumpay. Donald a maharajah! Replete with a harem and a small army (made up of three tired men, one of whom is a midget.) The catch? Apparently, Bumpay must pay its mortgage to Hoopadoola. To satisfy the bill, their maharajah must weigh the same or more than 100 pounds of diamonds, otherwise Hoopadoola takes Bumpay's finest tiger-hunting lands. Donald must weigh those 100 pounds (which he will unquestionably fail to do), or he'll get thrown to the tigers and Bumpay will wait until next year, when another victim is sacrificed to their mortgage.

Donald fails miserably, as we know he will. The kids rub gold dust into his feathers to weigh him down (still too light), then decide to shove a hose into their uncle's mouth and fill him with water just before he's weighed. However, they accidentally use a gas hose, causing Donald to fill up like a balloon. Put on the scale, it is determined that "He weighs less than nothing!" Jailed, waiting a sure death in the morning, Donald appears doomed. The boys are at a loss as to how to help save their uncle from being devoured. And then, walking the streets of Bumpay, they find the stub of a pencil, and another day of trading begins...

"Maharajah Donald" involves adventure and riotous slapstick, Donald a bumbling fool who steals his nephews treasures while desperately needing their help. Here, he is far from heroic—in fact, Donald is a coward and a thief, a man totally unwilling to work in this story and who floats through life like a feather, without enough weight literally and figuratively. Only the boys seem content to carve out their own path, and save their uncle in the meantime.

Were this a movie in the early career of an actor named Donald

Duck, "Maharajah Donald," despite having his name on the marquee, would not be considered one of his greatest, or even starring, roles. The kids are the stars here, and Donald, though fun, is really a tool for the boys to express their guile and intelligence.

The nephews' behavior is remarkable, not only are they totally resourceful, helping their uncle not only get to India, but save his life and bring him home, but they do so with total humility. Considering their treatment, one would think that at some point they would actually relish shoving a hose down their uncle's throat and filling him full of water. Rather, these ducks worry at first and then intently focus on the job at hand, the job of saving their uncle.

While "Maharajah Donald" works, it remains an early Barks story, and not quite up to par with later works. It's a bit clumsy in its exposition, the "editing," or sequencing of the story, isn't as sharp, and though it contains much of his hallmark style (locales, nephew v. uncle confrontations, Donald's anger); there's a ways to go before Barks reaches his zenith in terms of panel composition and backgrounds. All but one page is made up of eight similar panels, broken at times with a borderless panel with Donald or the boys circled for emphasis. And dull Burbank contrasts nicely with the (moderately) rich detail of India. Donald will grow as a more complex character as well, losing much of his nastiness and his cowardice.

The India of 1949's "Maharajah Donald" is a bit patronizing, but it was a stark contrast to the world of 1978, when I first read this story, many changes were taking place throughout the world. In India, for instance, 1974 marked the year the country exploded its first nuclear weapon, astonishingly called The Smiling Buddha, right near the border with Pakistan, and which sent shudders around the world.

So here we are, and the world is as complex as it has always been, but we can retreat to a so-called "simpler" time, when we believed that Indians and citizens from other nations didn't engage in the same complexities that we did. I like to believe that I'm after a solid story, and Barks delivers many of these. But how do we reconcile the racism, even if it's subtle? I mean, when I watch my favorite movies, like Hawks' *His Girl Friday*, it grates that there are overtly racist plot points. In that film, it was the fact that the escaped convict—who is supposed to be sympathetic, supposed to be funny—has killed a black police officer. In *His Girl Friday*, that murder is OK, and in fact what's awful is that the black community is demanding justice. Here, the racism is not so overt—in "Maharajah Donald" there are not so many ridiculous caricatures, and in fact the Indians have their own dignity and power and do not see the Ducks as being more privileged thanks to their being Americans.

So while I encourage readers to seek out Maharajah Donald, because it is a great story, an early "paper movie" of a great star, be aware of what you're reading, the work of a man who certainly didn't have much, if any contact, with Indians from the subcontinent. His understanding of the people was, again, imagination-based. Perhaps Barks should be praised for not making them even more of a caricature (less, even, than Apu, the Indian character from the more worldly *The Simpsons*.)

Fig. 4. Lost in the Andes, 2:1

# THE EGG AND I:
## Lost in the Andes

"Lost in the Andes" is widely regarded as Carl Barks' finest story, was his personal favorite, and the one he felt was his most technically perfect. Visually, it is an astonishing piece, taking us from cramped ship's quarters to the open sky above the mountains, through fog and bright sunlight, each panel masterfully rendered for maximum effect. As a story it is equally remarkable, personifying what critic Michael Barrier said of the auteur: "Barks was a writer first and an artist second, and his drawings have life because they are in the service of characters and ideas." This writing shines in "Lost in the Andes," taking us from a stuffy museum in Burbank, over a turbulent ocean to South America, up mountains, across plains, down valleys, and into a fog-shrouded land with strange people who speak like Southern Gentlemen from Alabama, with a heroic and curious Donald and brave and intelligent nephews who end up saving themselves from a life sentence in prison. For once, Donald is not motivated by greed or heroics, but curiosity and a taste for adventure. It is a morality play about happiness and a neat character study of the Ducks. Critics such as Thomas Andrae have examined "Lost in the Andes" and argued, quite effectively, that it possesses acidic criticisms of the capitalist system, that it deftly skewers the "myth of the explorer" and colonialism, while also

Fig. 5. Lost in the Andes, 2:1

managing to hold a mirror up to the closemindedness of preindustrial cultures, albeit ones that have been essentially colonialized. Like any masterpiece, "Lost in the Andes" means many things to many critics, each one finding something new with every reading.

But it is also a story about eggs.

Carl Barks was once an egg farmer, and this profession appears to have influenced more of his stories than any of his other failed efforts. Here, as in "The Magic Hourglass" (and a story not mentioned here, "Omelet", worth seeking out), eggs get things rolling. Even though these eggs don't roll.

"Lost in the Andes" begins quietly in a natural history museum, cleaning time at this hallowed institution. In the opening splash panel, we have a narrative box explaining that Donald is the fourth assistant janitor, and he's being ordered to clean by the third assistant janitor—a joke in and of itself, a stick in the eye to either the bloated bureaucracy of a major public museum, or to wage slaves and their need to be superior to someone, anyone. Donald wears the eager look of a man intent on his work. His superior seems like a total jerk. Our hero's assignment? To polish stones.

From this lowly moment in Donald's life the adventure begins. Donald is supposed to clean years of accumulated dust on "ancient Inca ruins," including what appear to be square stones. Here, Donald's clumsiness is a boon: he drops one of these stones, and is shocked to discover it breaks open on the floor, spilling its contents. The rocks, as it turns out, are eggs. By the end of page two we will see Donald and his nephews aboard an expeditionary boat to Peru, and along the way there's a sudden, breakneck pace to Barks' paper movie, the montage of discovery.

"Donald's accidental discovery startles the scientific world!" In a wonderful, page-wide panel, Barks shows eleven scientists studying and arguing over the eggs. (see Fig. 5) What a collection of, well, eggheads. They are bearded in most cases (including one fellow who is nothing but a pair of eyes in the midst of a shrub of facial hair), though the one who is not stares at the others through a pair of bottle-thick specs and has nothing but wrinkles, like a shar pei. In the next panel, a pair of fat, egg-headed, wealthy "egg dealers" (with diamonds on their shirts), are literally drooling with anticipation of what these eggs can do for their industry (and the fact that one of them fondles a square egg suggests that the scientists' forthcoming journey is going to be underwritten by these unpleasant people.) Next, we see a pair of rube chicken farmers "agog" (in Barks' words) over the possibilities as well.

One of the things I've always loved about Barks is his attention to background detail, and especially the jokes he puts in the form of signs and shapes. In the panel with the fat-cats fondling the square hen fruit, you'll notice there's a graph with the name "Interglobal Eggs—'Something to Cackle About!'" on the wall, and the globe in their office is egg shaped. As the farmers yak on about the possible bounty of "square fryers with round corners," one of the roosters is looking on, sweat flying from his brow. The ships, the offices, the farms are rich with this background detail, but detail that helps us slow down to appreciate each panel of the story.

Once everyone gets on the boat, we see a reprisal of the hierarchy that existed at the museum, a system that Donald will be free from thanks, again, to eggs. The discovery of the square eggs released

Fig. 6. Lost in the Andes, 3:2

Donald from the walls of the museum, as he is hauled along on this expedition with only his nephews beneath him in the pecking order. In a weird but hilarious sequence, the top scientist demands an omelet from his assistant, Tombsbury. He, in turn, demands his assistant, Wormsley, make it instead (in a panel that has a strange noirish tilt to it, shot from a god's-eye-point-of-view and looking like a lost frame from Orson Welles' *Lady From Shanghai*). (see Fig. 6) Wormsley, without any of the dignity he or his supervisor received, shouts at Donald, whose name he doesn't even know--"Hey you! The prof wants an omelet! Get busy!" Our hero, chest puffed out, calls for "Assistants Four, Five, and Six…" to make the omelet. These are, of course, Huey, Dewey and Louie, who are all blowing gum bubbles.

Like the pencil stub in "Maharajah Donald," the nephews' gum bubbles are a clue to a future solution. Without finding any eggs, the boys use what's available, and follow orders, making an omelet from the square eggs—you know, the eggs that are decades old.

As the plate of rancid omelet is handed off from assistant to assistant, each man, hungry I guess, takes a small bite, and by page five each and every member of this expedition—with the exception of the nephews—is sick beyond belief (with "Acute Ptomaine Ptosis of the Ptummy!"). When the ship finally lands in Peru, the same hierarchical chain rejects the idea of chasing after square eggs, having lost interest thanks to their sickness. Donald, being near the bottom, thinks to send his nephews, but decides to go himself when he sees them blowing bubbles. Apparently he believes that he's the only one mature enough to lead this expedition.

Outside of the thrill of watching this story unfold, of the madness of square eggs and the rather ridiculous way the expedition has at once unraveled and sent our hero on his way, what strikes me as significant here is Donald's motivation. Though we know that Donald is going to fumble and bumble along the way, much to our joy, he's also a much richer character now than he was in, say, "Maharajah Donald." He's someone with direction, brave, pushing through to find the source of those square eggs. Do we think to ask why? Consider: as Thomas Andrae points out in his remarkable *Carl Barks and the Disney Comic Book*, Donald has never received credit for the initial discovery of the eggs (not that accidentally dropping one while cleaning is worthy of tremendous accolades), but Barks has pretty much established that Donald isn't going to get anything more than his day's wages for this dangerous journey—wages which I can't imagine amounts to much.

And yet, in the treacherous mountains of Peru, Donald and the nephews push on, despite numerous failings (all of which are funny), even going so far as to climb to the "the highest plateau in the region!" and then, "[m]iles and miles and miles later," feeling more frustrated than exhausted, the clan comes across a very old fellow who speaks of an American who passed through and into the "region of the mists." This American returned with "a look of madness," cold and hungry. Armed with this news, the ducks practically race into the mists, even as the old man tries to call them back to warn them that no one but that American had ever returned.

What's amazing to me is that we're not even at the heart of this story, and already so many great things have occurred. The ducks plunge into fog (in perhaps the only section of the book I don't find all that visually intriguing—Barks rendered the ducks in the fog as dark lines, to represent the difficulty of seeing them, but they all come off as stiff.) Our heroes slide down a grassy slope and into a warm valley, where the fog thins out and everyone can see suddenly. And there is perhaps Barks' best splash panel (see Plate 2): "A lost world beneath the fog!" Donald whispers (I assume), and an amazing panorama (which Barks claimed he screwed up, perspective-wise, though it's very hard to notice). "Every bit of it is built with square blocks," Donald notes.

Once down the slope, Donald and his nephews again bravely confront a new culture, men and women with squarish heads, boxy noses, and speaking, inexplicably at first, in a southern accent. In fact, the first "native" they encounter is singing "Dixie", one of the most charged songs a person could imagine hearing from the mouth of a lost culture from South America.

Turns out this is the city of Plain Awful, and these are the "Awfultonians," living in an Inca-inspired, fog-shrouded paradise where the only cuisine is eggs prepared in the usual way—fried, poached, scrambled, boiled. And yet, no chickens. Ushered to the dining table of the President, the ducks fear they're going to be eaten, but really this is the Awfultonians serving our heroes dinner and showing off their "Southern Hospitality." Barks likes to throw in weird little asides, such as one of the nephews (hat free, so who knows who's saying what?) stating "I hope we have filets of spring vicuna with wild rice dressing!" What? No, kids, you're getting eggs, and here Barks' comic timing asserts itself. As Donald peppers the Prez with question after question, interspersed within this dialogue is the kids' own deflating expectations as course after course of eggs comes their way ("Second course... scrambled sggs!") (see Fig. 7) Turns out an explorer, the "Professor from Birmingham" (Alabama, natch, and spelled phonetically: "Bummin'ham"), "discovered" this

Fig. 7. Lost in the Andes, 21:8

ancient city. Such was his influence, apparently, that the whole culture accepted his name for the place (Plain Awful), took his language, took his accent, took his favorite music and even took his country's system of government, as they have a President, make the Ducks Secretaries of Agriculture, etc. So while the U.S. doesn't seek to colonialize, our imperialist system of setting up submissive democracies exists even in Barks' universe.

But where do these eggs come from? Themes repeat themselves in "Lost in the Andes:" the ducks discover the source of the eggs, square chickens that look like rocks. They find them when the boys blow a gum bubble and stick it to a square boulder, which turns out to be the slumbering fowls, who react angrily. When they're rewarded with their appointments to Secretaries of Agriculture, the boys reveal how they discovered the birds, and the Awfultonians freak out: round bubbles in a square culture? Blasphemy! The boys have violated the "only law" (no one steals or kills here). "It is chiseled in th' statutes that whoevah projuces a round object mus' spend the rest of his life in th' stone quarries!" the President proclaims. Because of their heroics, they get a second chance: the boys must blow square bubbles.

Round vs. square, chicken and egg. Needless to say, the boys succeed, but even after this success, how do they escape Plain Awful and get back home? Well, it was the museum that set them on this journey, and it is a museum that sends them on their way back—the museum of Plain Awful has on display a compass, which the ducks trade for square dance lessons (which is, of course, a dance performed in a variety of circles.)

Emerging from the fog, our heroes pause, with a pair of chickens in a case on their backs, and reflect on the happiness of the Awfultonians, people who, Donald notes, have "never seen the sun," but "were the happiest people we have ever known."

So why not stay? Well, if we go by the rules of the Campbellian hero's journey, our man must return to his own culture, return with the spoils of his quest. For once, Donald expects to get some credit—in fact, we see him radioing the museum from the ship, sitting at the table with the scientists as they study his chickens, proud of his accomplishment that will change the poultry industry forever... until one hilarious mistake upends this entire expedition.

Again: the question that plagues me is "why?" Why is this lowly factotum pushing himself and his nephews—up mountains, into a "lost world," and back again—on this maniacal quest for square eggs? Yes, "Lost in the Andes" can be seen, as Andrae so eloquently states, as a critique of capitalism and Donald's vast failures, his inability to make money or find success. But this is the thrust behind the Barks' Donald Duck comics as a whole I think—that Donald is someone who just wants more out of his life, which I find exhilarating and inspirational. As a child, we gape and marvel at the opportunities afforded to the nephews, and something so childish—gum bubbles—both push the kids into peril and get them out of the same. For adults caught in meaningless jobs, Donald represents that heroic dream—that some happy accident will come along when we least expect it, and send us on a journey. Donald has no illusions that he's not going to make any money, or at least doesn't speak of any kind of remuneration. Instead, he presses forward, for the thrill of adventure.

This is what Donald does for us, but perhaps most importantly, perhaps this is what he did for Carl Barks himself. The man was paid all of $925 for his work in that comic book, $800 of which represented his payment for "Lost in the Andes." *Walt Disney's Comics and Stories* usually sold close to three million copies, but let's be conservative and say that issue sold only a cool million—that means Barks commanded a sweet nine ten-thousandths of a cent per issue (had Disney given him just a half cent per issue, Barks would have made five grand by the same estimation, which would have no doubt made him insanely happy.) By this time (1949), Barks was barely making it as a writer/ illustrator for Western Comics, was sinking in the morass of a second, disastrous marriage (to a drunk), with a pair of daughters from the first bad marriage and few prospects outside of this work. Armed with that stack of *National Geographics* and an *Encyclopedia Brittanica*, trying desperately to forget the living hell of his domestic life, he created in his hero an everyman who could do what he could not—escape. Certainly, he critiqued capitalist hierarchy, and used this Inca-like culture to his benefit. He shared with us his need for escape, revealing that the journey is its own reward.

Fig. 8. The Gilded Man, 29:1

There is virtually no one who likes Gladstone Gander. Well, that may not actually be true—specifically, *I* don't like him, and no one I know who loves these comics likes this character, either. In fact, liking this wretched creature is something I would probably hold against you. According to critic Geoffrey Blum, even Carl Barks loathed the lucky goose, who is the catalyst of both "Luck of the North" and "The Gilded Man," two of my favorite stories that work in spite of this beaked annoyance. According to Blum, Barks hated how Gladstone essentially destroyed narrative. The "lucky" duck, or goose, is clad in a bow tie, bright blue jacket, gray hat tipped back and covering his curly gray locks, which makes him look strangely like Joseph Cotton, and gets anything that he wants, all the time. "Gladstone represents the guy who curdles everyone's cream," Barks complained in an interview. "He is the wavy-haired dandy who always has a better car than ours, a prettier girlfriend, an easier time in life. My wife despises him." There's very little you can do with this type of character, but also because, let's be honest, he's kind of dumb. Plus, I don't agree that he's the guy we all hate because he gets everything. There are people who we believe have been given all the breaks in life—those we might characterize as being born with a silver spoon in their mouth—but the reality is that they are still real people. Each human suffers, even the rich jerks we can't stand, at the very least from their own mortality and probably plain human loneliness.

Gladstone and Donald are, of course, free from life's decay, but Gladstone usually gets everything he wants with such a grotesque ease that he's boring. What's more, isn't it unfathomable that he himself would want to live his life like this? Gladstone wakes, and everything is given to him. He doesn't have to strive for anything. Barks, inexplicably, shows us a Gladstone who is not like Midas, but a man who is blissfully happy to get all of life's treasures dumped in his lap.

I've included "Luck of the North" primarily because of Gladstone's presence, but also because this is a weird adventure that pushes Donald to do very weird things, and I think it's fun. Here, and in "The Gilded Man," we have two stories in which our hero collides with a Trickster God in the form of Gladstone. We're starting to see the bent panels that became a hallmark of Barks' style, and the action is brilliant, without a single wasted panel. In "Luck," the Ducks are sent on a rescue mission of their (actually Donald's) own making. In "The Gilded Man," Gladstone is both an impediment but also the key to getting Donald out of Duckburg and on the road to British Guiana. Which is a good thing.

Let's start with "Luck of the North." Typically, Barks contained Gladstone in the short "ten pagers" from the *Walt Disney's Comics and Stories* magazine, little distractions that are akin to, say, two-reelers in the silent era. Little plot and a lot of slapstick and jokes are Gladstone's usual terrain. Theoretically, the contrast between Gladstone's good and Donald's bad luck made for great humor. Not the least of which is that Donald's luck seems entirely human and Gladstone's just seems weird, almost godly.

Luck works, despite the fact that Barks takes forever to get his story off the ground. If you think Gladstone sounds like a laugh riot, well,

Fig. 9. Luck of the North, 21:8

then you get a perfect sampler of his kind of story in the first eight pages of this tale. He runs into Donald and then inexplicably follows him around for a few hours. We get a venerable buffet of good fortune, as Gladstone runs into a bill collector (and manages to make five bucks), buys a trunk for fifty cents at an auction (and finds a hundred dollars), buys a single ticket at a Benefit Bazaar for Blue Cats ("Help Buy Red Dye for Blue Cats!") (see Fig. 9) and wins a gold watch. And so on, and so on, and so on.

Irritated, Donald falsifies a map of a uranium mine, picking some coordinates out of nowhere, sending his cousin Gladstone, as it were, on a wild goose chase. Donald leaves it on the sidewalk, where Gladstone finds the map and takes off. Later, Donald checks the globe—he's sent his cousin out to the Bering Sea! He laughs heartily, and then, in the night, begins to regret his joke. Thinking about Gladstone trapped on an iceberg, Donald tosses and turns in bed and then says "Wonder if he thought to take a knife and fork—or am I being funny?" He then realizes that he has to go save his cousin from certain death, rounding up his nephews and taking off for the northernmost reaches of Alaska.

I find this story amusing, even as it makes no Goddamn sense whatsoever, even within its own logic. For starters, Gladstone, as he's been established (and as you will see later in "The Gilded Man"), hates work. Much of this was determined in later stories, but it's also pretty evident in earlier short works featuring Gladstone. In fact, there's a ten pager whose culminating joke is that Gladstone keeps a dime hidden away in a giant safe, kept out of view because he's ashamed that he once earned money working. In other Gladstone stories, he outright rejects good fortune if it involves any kind of labor on his part. Under no circumstances would this dude drop everything to fly north, equip himself with sled dogs in a tiny Alaskan hamlet, and then sail in the frigid Bering Sea to earn millions. (And let us set aside the fact that even by Gladstone's low standards, you would have to be monumentally idiotic to think there's a mine of any metal in the middle of the sea.)

Admittedly, Barks would probably grouse at me that there's no continuity in his stories (which is actually a real strength) and that here Gladstone works a bit. Fair enough, except that in the Barks universe everyone has continuity but Donald and his nephews. Still, a man can change his mind. But Gladstone also doesn't need millions. Even here he gets everything he wants with no effort. Why does he want the headaches of wealth when anything he wants—money, food, shelter (though presumably not companionship)—are his at the snap of a finger? (Nor would he borrow money from a loan shark—as seen in the second page of this story—but that's a nitpick on my part.)

This leads me to another aside, one of my favorite elements of all of Barks' Duck stories. These are all family stories, in the sense that they're about a family, the Duck family. Notice: it's never just Donald Duck racing here or there to do this or that, but Donald and his Nephews. If you're a kid this is pure magic. Think about "Luck of the North" for a minute: Donald cannot sleep, tosses and turns, and finally decides to rescue not only an adult, but the luckiest fucking adult that ever lived from certain death. I don't know about you, but if I had children, hauling them along to the Bering Sea is the last thing I'd do.

Fig. 9. Luck of the North, 10:6

And yet, he does, and this is amazing. Donald Duck and his nephews aren't cloying, there's rarely if ever that stickly-sweet moment where we see these as helpless children. More a team than a modern family, the ducks are adventurers all.

Only in "Maharajah Donald," a very early comic, does Donald even entertain the idea of not bringing the kids along. As a child, you appreciate this notion that whenever adventure's to be had, whenever danger rears its head, an adult turns to you for help. Thomas Andrae points out that "in facing danger, the ducks become protective and helpful to one another." This is stark contrast to the cartoons and earlier versions, in which the kids basically went berserk, then Donald goes berserk, and in theory we all go berserk with laughter. In fact, we barely get the feeling that these are kids, until later in "Luck of the North" when Donald tries to convince Gladstone to take the kids with him from a floating iceberg (which the nephews refuse to do.)

Barks is in his element here, sending us zooming to a small hamlet above the Arctic Circle, where our heroes run into trouble almost immediately. First, the town held a raffle for a dogsled, and of course

Gladstone won the sled and is well on his way to the coast. Either because they haven't money, or there wasn't another dogsled, Donald hitches the kids up to a sled (see Fig. 9). Barks paints this frozen world as terribly brutal but thrilling. Cutting away to show the village as nestled in mountains, and the fact that the ducks are either moving at 45 degree angles, or heads-down against the snow and wind almost makes the reader shiver with them.

Donald eventually catches up with Gladstone, sneaking up and stealing what he thinks is the map from under his cousin's sleeping head, only to discover it wasn't the map. This is essential, because it communicates to Gladstone that someone is on his trail, and so he'll do what he can to thwart the pursuer. However, again, it doesn't actually make a lot of sense—why didn't Donald just confront Gladstone (as happens later)?

From here, Gladstone stumbles across some very realistic Eskimos, which I'm guessing Barks copied from a January 1947 edition of *National Geographic*, and perhaps his own copy of *Encyclopedia Britannica*. They're hungry, starved for whale meat. Gladstone wants to buy a kayak and get to his floating mine. Unwilling to sell, Gladstone convinces them to trade the two kayaks in their possession for a good luck charm that'll bring in the whales. In an amazing half-page splash panel (see Plate 3), with one corner carved out to show a profile of Gladstone nervously shaking a tin horseshoe at the water, we see a big blue whale leap onto the beach. And with that, Gladstone kayaks away, leaving the other one torn to pieces.

When Donald arrives, after the Eskimos have failed to summon more whales, and are subsequently angry (and probably alarmed that they now have absolutely zero methods by which to hunt wales). demand from our man that he "pony up the price of one whale!"— sixty-five dollars—in exchange for the kayak. Undaunted, the ducks repair their kayak (How? Never mind...) and set out to the Bering Sea after their stupid cousin.

And now we begin to see the growth of Donald the "star" of Barks' "novels," as he called them, or "paper movies," as I do. Gone is the lowlife of "Maharajah Donald," gone, even, is the wide-eyed plebian who stumbles into a magic land in "Lost in the Andes." Once engaged in the most challenging part of the adventure, "Luck of the North," suddenly shows Donald in possession of a tremendous amount of strength, intelligence, and capability (even more than we've already seen.) Donald and the boys are not only adept at rowing this kayak through turbulent seas, but Donald is skilled at using a sextant. "The polar seas are full of dangers," Barks writes in a narration panel above an image of Donald surveying the horizon, "but stout hearts and firm minds can conquer all!" And here the story becomes focused, charged, and totally thrilling. Visually, the sea engaged Barks like nothing else. Upon reaching the water, "Luck" shifts from an 8-panel grid, to fewer visually arresting splash panels that break the page as an iceberg breaks the horizon. A regular sized panel (which conforms to the earlier 8-panel grid) in a corner, connects the narrative to the larger and more impressive wide shot. Each of these commands the eye, propelling the reader through the story—we're going to see a whale leaping on shore! A giant iceberg! A sinking ship! (see Plates 3 and 4)

Whenever I read these Donald Duck comics as a child, loafing on my bedroom floor, ignoring the world outside, it was akin to being in a theater. I saw the larger panels as grandiose shots, wide-angle Cinemascope marvels of the Bering Sea. Barks' use of close-ups, long-distance images, and skewed panels—rectangles bending about on the page to direct the eye toward the most dramatic point on the page—make these read cinematically, moving with the same pace as a great action film.

Donald finally connects with Gladstone, who is trying to find uranium on an iceberg with a Geiger counter (yes, you read that right—it's amazing that a moving iceberg would stay on that spot).

Upon confronting one another, the two hotheads fight, and in the process sink Gladstone's kayak, leaving only Donald's with its four seats. They flip a coin to see who will go for rescue, and of course the lucky one wins. This is where Donald demands Gladstone haul the kids along, but when they scatter, refusing to leave Donald, Gladstone takes off. As he rows away, he sees, in a page wide panel, a Viking ship frozen in the berg (see Plate 4).

The Ducks endure. Left with a fishing line (but no drinking water) they eat raw fish, and the nephews appear fatigued and emaciated as the story goes on (nice work dragging them along, Mr. Duck.) As the winds blow them into warmer seas, making large chunks of the ice fall into the sea, Donald wonders aloud "if help comes for us, how will they ever recognize this berg?" with its now totally different exterior. To make matters worse, a warship begins using their frozen island for target practice. Explosions tear into the berg, it splits in half, and in a small yet emotionally charged panel, we see a silhouette of the ducks, holding hands, falling to their deaths, and saying "Good-bye Unca' Donald." (see Fig. 9)

Because I'm hoping you'll seek these stories out, I'll keep you from too much of the finish, except to say that our boys land on the Viking

Fig. 10. Luck of the North, 23:7

ship, manage to get rescued by Gladstone, who takes all the valuable gold on board, and leaves them behind (at their angry request.) With a sleek Viking ship to take them home, they encounter even more disaster, but emerge with a strange sort of wealth—a real Viking map, worth "many times more than the gold that Gladstone got from the Viking ship." They're rescued by the Coast Guard at the end, who remark that the ducks are out of their head, singing,

> *Gladstone's luck*
> *Ain't worth a shuck*
> *It takes a duck*
> *To have good luck!*

We'll see that this is equally true in "The Gilded Man," a story that is just as adventurous, but also as economically satisfying for the Ducks as "Luck of the North."

Let's open with the splash panel, of Donald, at his desk, which is crowded with multi-color books. Huge books, fat as telephone directories, but these are albums and catalogues of rare stamps. On the wall is a huge map of South America, with one country highlighted—British Guiana (as today's Guyana was known then.) Donald's lost in his work, and his word balloon communicates a bundle: "Three Blue Centennials worth ten cents apiece, and a Belgian Prince Leopold worth four bucks!" As usual, Barks' storytelling chops come shining through: from the map, we know where we're going, and from that word balloon, we know why. Though the title is "The Gilded Man," this is a hunt for a rare stamp.

The backstory comes at us quickly, in a very sweet panel as the boys want their uncle to take them to a movie. First let me say that one of the hallmarks of the Donald Duck stories is the home, a warm and comfortable place. Barks never really put a ton of detail into this modest space, but over time I've come to see it has a living room, kitchen, bathroom, dining room, a bedroom for the uncle and one for Huey, Duey and Louie, and an office. Over the years, and in other comics, we see a tiny garage with Donald's little red roadster convertible (with its "313" license plate), and a yard in which Donald was forever struggling to grow a garden (or the battlefield for the combat with Neighbor Jones, from a series of hilarious ten-pagers.)

First of all, the way the nephews ask their uncle to see a movie is adorable—this was a time period when these kids could go on their own, walk all over town if they felt like it, but they want Donald to take them to a movie. The Duck home serves to ground Donald and the kids, give them the weight of a place they call their own. It is Donald's as much as it is theirs, and I think its lack of detail was Barks' way of making it everyone's home (and in stark contrast to Uncle Scrooge's money bin, with all its dollar sign imagery on every surface, where the old man spends all his time, and which is no one's home.)

Donald denies the kids' request, as he is too busy working on his stamp collection. After some wiseacre remarks from the kids, he points out that he is in pursuit of the rarest of stamps, from British Guiana. Now, I don't know if Barks intended to do this or not, but this Macguffin (Hitchcock's term for the device that sets your hero—or the bad guys—off on a journey, like the water in *Chinatown*, pornography in *The Big Sleep*, or stamps here) is a mystery for some time: the specific name of the stamp is not mentioned once until page 11, almost a third of the way through, as if to suggest that it's not worth worrying about. In fact, it is the eponymous gilded man who will make this story really sing, and whose presence is also a mystery until that same page.

"The Gilded Man" is a story about the pursuit of financial success, and we know that from the opening splash panel. Donald explains to the perplexed nephews that his collecting is not for the joy of the stamp itself, but so that he can save enough to go to Guiana, and find a rare One Cent Magenta Stamp of 1856. (see Fig. 11) Once found, Donald simply plans to sell the stamp, rather than collect it himself.

Fig. 11. The Gilded Man, 1:5

Let's back up a bit to examine the beginning of the path of what will be one of the weirdest plot devices to move a story along. Barks once said, of his training at Disney's cartoon combine, that "I would have to say that the key was, you have to have a reason for everything. If you could find a reason for something, you could drag anything in [to your story.]" After the boys are schooled about the One Cent Magenta Stamp of 1856, we cut to Donald digging through the wastebaskets at the Duckburg train station, looking for, and finding, moderately rare stamps. Gladstone comes upon his cousin, makes a snide remark, and then Donald, not thinking, spills the beans about the rare stamp and how much money he plans to make. Naturally, Gladstone finds a whole damn stamp album on a seat in the station.

Alarmed at the rarity of the stamps, Donald forces Gladstone to take it to its owner, one Philo T. Ellic (har, har, "philatelic" is the term for the study of stamps), where Gladstone expects a bundle in a reward. And, as we know, he gets it. A thousand bucks—enough, Donald says in exasperation, to get him to British Guiana.

Money in hand, Gladstone makes a hasty retreat from Ellic's home

Fig. 12. The Gilded Man, 8:5

(and the story), and then Donald, destitute, collapses in the easy chair in Ellic's office and mopes as the millionaire occupies himself with his stamp collection. As a child, and today, I find this monumentally discomforting—Donald and Gladstone are strangers, and in this man's home, and when Gladstone leaves, and thus ending any reason for them to stay, Donald remains sitting, staring into space while the guy ignores him. It's weird. Nonetheless, Ellic looks up, startled, and wonders just who is this guy sitting in his office. Well, Ellic is what we might call today a victim of dementia—he remembered virtually nothing about leaving his stamps behind, that he paid Gladstone a reward, or that Donald is just the guy who came with him. Thinking Donald brought back the collection, he gives him a thousand bucks, and when Donald tries to give it back, Ellic believes our man's being confoundedly noble, and has his servant not only boot Donald out of the mansion, but to make sure "he keeps that money!"

And with that, they're off, on a journey to find that stamp and make that money. But there's a significant panel before they reach their destination. Sailing on a ship, the boys read up on Guiana, and speak of El Dorado, the legendary Gilded Man. It is a brief moment, out of nowhere really, but it leads us to the next act of this journey, when the real motive of Donald's quest makes itself apparent: the thrill of adventure. In perhaps the most significant panel not just here but maybe the whole of Barks' canon, we see Donald, smiling, staring out to sea and saying "Oh, well, if we don't find anything, we'll have a lot of fun looking!" (see Fig. 12)

Interestingly enough, the next two pages show that looking is actually not a lot of fun. But this is the pursuit of a stamp, and not for the stamp's intrinsic beauty, but for the $50,000 this stamp is worth. After a week of futility, the boys are loafing by the Orinico River (as stated in an earlier panel, even though that river doesn't flow though Guiana) when they see an old man's dugout swamped by a speedboat. He falls into the river and screams for help, as piranhas, inexplicably called by the poor man "Cannibal Fish!" (which would mean he's safe since they eat only other piranhas?), set upon devouring him. Thinking quickly, one of the boys throws a bottle of castor oil at the man, who douses himself in the stuff, as the cannibal fish make faces and back away.

Exhausted, the old man thanks the boys and tells them he will do anything for them, such is his gratitude. The boys tell him to "skip it,"

Fig. 13. The Gilded Man, 11:2

then ask him if he knows where to find the One Cent Magenta Stamp of 1856, in the first instance the stamp is mentioned by name.

Like "Lost in the Andes," we see Barks relying on an old man to allow our heroes entrance into a magical otherworld that no one else has found. Animals also help on this journey. As the Ducks march into the jungles, carrying a rifle (which Barks, unlike Chekov, decided to keep unfired), they rely on a tame monkey to lead them to the promised land.

Almost immediately, they find what they're looking for—a leather mail pouch with silver belt buckles—but in doing so infuriate the enormous El Dorado, who stands before them, nearly naked, and a human being, to boot. Typically, Barks depicted everyone as an animal of sorts, usually dog-like; their canine nature revealed only by black noses and floppy ears (they have flesh colored faces and hands, and no tails, unlike Donald and his family). But here, El Dorado and his men are, in fact, men, which actually lends an added air of menace to the whole scene—something about those dog faces are none too threatening.

Donald and the boys are captured, thrown into a dungeon beneath the temple, and are going to be sacrificed in the morning. I won't reveal the details of their escape, except to say that it involves the nephews, once again saving their uncle, and, strangely, making El Dorado one happy dude.

What happens next is a strange conclusion, one that I think befits his interactions with Gladstone. The Donald Duck comics are, as I've mentioned, about journeys, about the joys or risk-taking and the spiritual success of such travels. However, "The Gilded Man," as in Luck of the North, is one of the few stories where Donald's success is purely financial, for even though we've had a rip-roaring adventure as readers, Donald for once seems not to care that he encountered the great mystery of the story, in this case El Dorado. Where usually he will pause to reflect upon his journey, here Donald is interested solely in the stamps, and even then not for any reason other than it's cash value. In fact, we never end up seeing the stamp, which I think is a wasted opportunity from many angles, not the least of which you could perhaps show it as being unbelievably ugly or dull. But the stamp was of zero importance even to Barks—money is the focal point here.

On the verge of boarding a steamer home, Donald is stopped at customs, where the prized mail pouch is seized by a government inspector (the English government by the way—this is still colonialized South America.) This bag, after all, remains the property of the King, and it must be delivered. A sympathetic postal employee allows Donald to write down the address and follow it—if the woman who is to receive the letter in question is still around, "Perhaps you can recover the letter from her."

To this day, I still don't quite get what "recovering" the letter from "Miss Susiebell Swan" would mean. It's a sure bet that someone from 1856 is probably long dead by 1952, when this story was released. Surely, Donald's not interested in offering her a fair price for the stamp. He just wants to get his grubby feathers on it so he can sell to someone else. Well, Donald follows the stamp, from Mudhen, Ohio,

Fig. 14. The Gilded Man, 29:4

where Miss Swan is no longer living, to Webfoot, Oregon, where she had a forwarding address. In Webfoot, which is a city so perpetually flooded that taxis drive through waist-deep water and the postman wears waders, Donald discovers that Miss Swan "floated away in 1901" to Duckburg.

This is actually terrible news. Back home, our heroes race to the post office, only to get there just when—guess who?—Gladstone is coming to pick up his mail. And so the story circles back: Gladstone gets the stamp, realizes its value (thanks in no small part to Donald's earlier gloating, which of course got him the money to go to Guiana, which brings us here) and races to Mr. Philo T. Ellic to sell. The Ducks inexplicably follow him, and stare forlornly as the monster emerges, $50,000 richer.

Shooing the kids because he wants to take a long walk alone, Donald will stop every ten feet to "have a tantrum" (we see him running his head into a wall in frustration.) This was Barks' reflection on Donald's bad luck—only, as we will see, his luck will turn, albeit in a weird, and perhaps unethical way. For Donald, destitute on a bridge, is in the right place at the right time, as Philo T. Ellic, absent-minded to the extreme, hails a taxi right next to Donald, and then proceeds to leave the album with the valuable stamp on the railing, right next to our man.

On a train that Ellic believes is bound for San Francisco (actually it's a train to Chicago—and Ellic's bad memory is now about as much fun as Mr. Magoo's blindness), Donald hops aboard. Just when Ellic is about to panic at losing the album, Donald appears, and he receives a $50,000 reward.

I guess Ellic gave Donald the value of the stamp since he actually saved a whole book's full of rare stamps. But the conclusion here goes against the grain of most of Barks' stories—namely, that the money doesn't matter, it's the fun of the journey, the thrill of adventure and learning that makes life worth living.

Perhaps Barks was hamstrung by the character of Gladstone. For Donald seems continually in battle with his cousin, when it would seem like the best route would be to leave him alone. In a sense, you can't beat Gladstone, any more than you can beat luck in general. Specifically, Donald's victories in "Maharajah Donald," "Lost in the Andes," and the other stories we'll examine are not very measurable in terms of hard dollars. Barks has to tread lightly on "beating" Gladstone philosophically, as that could only be communicated through some kind of cloying speech. With Gladstone in the picture, Donald can only win by getting more (or an equal amount of) treasure, as he does here and in "Luck of the North."

That said, both are ripping adventure yarns, and the details again served Barks well. Donald's following the Magenta stamp from Ohio to Oregon to California is brisk, and Barks wisely made each and every visit radically different—in Mudhen, time has stood still, as the post office is covered in cobwebs, and a weird little robot stamps letters; in Webfoot the water permeates everything; back in Duckburg, in a weird coincidence that I'm not sure was intentional, the postman looks identical to the one in Webfoot—wearing an Amish style beard, glasses, lacking only the pipe of the other. The South American backgrounds are rich with detail, vines growing around and inside homes. Donald is, once again, as ridiculous as he is heroic.

But can we really say, as Barks and other critics have, that Donald is unlucky? He is the one stamp collector in the whole world who is able to find this stamp. We open with his dream of finding a stamp, sequestered as he is in his office, and the story will basically take us to where he achieves his goal, which really was to obtain $50,000. Along with the reward, he and his nephews not only found the stamp, but as an aside uncovered El Dorado, the mythical Gilded Man. If that's unlucky, I'm curious to know Barks' idea of good luck. Gladstone's mind-numbingly endless fortune? No thanks.

Fig. 15. The Magic Hourglass, 13:7

## THE EVIL THAT MEN DO:
### *The Magic Hourglass*

Let me admit something: I think Uncle Scrooge is a jerk. "The Magic Hourglass" will only prove this point if I'm willing to ignore every other Scrooge comic in existence. For whatever reason, Carl Barks thought very highly of the old man, and readers have come to agree. As I've stated, I do actually like some of the Scrooge comics. But I have to confess to being prejudiced against the wealthy in general, and this certainly affects my impression of the old duck.

I honestly cannot comprehend wanting to read the "heroic" Scrooge McDuck again and again. His Money Bin is an oppressive, depressing place, with its fat piles of cash and coin, dollar signs everywhere, nothing of beauty anywhere, just a place for a miser to hoard the world's wealth. Scrooge has no friends, no companions, just scared sycophants and brow-beaten opponents. At various times enemies swoop in to steal his fortune or challenge his status as the wealthiest man on earth. Really: who doesn't root for the Beagle Boys in their pursuit? Or wish that someone, anyone, would beat this old miser? Too often gifts to the poor have to be tricked out of him, and even then he seems pained, as if by a stomach ailment, to release even a damn dime. Yes, in the parlance of today's trickle-down economics, Scrooge creates jobs, but no one is empowered by these, rather, they're browbeaten into submission. Duckburg with Scrooge is not the Duckburg that Donald lives in when Scrooge is absent—it's a place controlled by the man, who seems, on many occasions, to literally possess every industry in town (and in other comics, the whole world).

"The Magic Hourglass" is included here because this is the one time Barks really emphasized Scrooge's shortcomings. For once he suggests that the old bastard is in fact a horrible person; Scrooge is lonely, and unable to grasp the joys and beauty of life. Scrooge loses here. He loses big, selling his soul for wealth.

But "The Magic Hourglass" also succeeds because our heroes embark on yet another of their crazy journeys, trying to refill a magic hourglass in the mystical sands from the Oasis of No Issa, sailing across the Atlantic in a broken-down boat that is powered—get this— by a pair of great white sharks, show themselves to be able gunmen, and finally, in a nod to Frank Norris' McTeague, end up discovering the true meaning of wealth and water.

Barks' talents were on full display here, both visually and in terms of storytelling. A magnificent splash panel opens this story, of the Ducks staring out from the observation deck of a skyscraper out over a curving river that cuts through a downtown of tall buildings and ferry terminals. (see Plate 6) This is now Duckburg, not Burbank, and this vibrant skyline resembles Chicago. "What a swell view of the city!" the nephews proclaim. "You mean a swell view of some of my Uncle Scrooge's property!" Donald retorts, and we know instantly that most of the city is owned by Uncle Scrooge. An argument ensues between them, the nephews and Donald quarreling over which one Uncle Scrooge likes the best.

Cut to Scrooge in his smoking jacket, cooking his breakfast—alone, of course. He carries on an interior monologue about an hourglass he uses to time his boiled "hen fruit" just right—three minutes to perfection. "Not once has it failed to tell the time exactly! Not once in all the years since I bought it in a thieves' market in Morocco!"

And then... whoops! When cracked, the eggs spill out on the plate, undercooked. That rotten hourglass' sand has worn out. In a foul mood, Scrooge reads his financial reports over his lousy eggs, and discovers something troubling: a fishing boat, the "Junk II" is worthless and draining money from the Scrooge McDuck corporation.

"Thus does destiny's scheme begin to hatch!" reads the narration box above the next panel, and again we see the mysterious power of eggs in a Barks narrative. Scrooge calls his nephews and Donald to his office, as he says, with a smile on his wicked face, "to show you how much I love you!" Is this the only mention of the word "love" in the whole of the Barks' canon? Maybe, maybe not, but it stands out here like a sore thumb. In Disney comics in general, this loaded word of affection is rarely used, such is its power, just as there's few parents, husbands and wives, just a collection of uncles, aunts, and boyfriend and girlfriends. Scrooge, trying to get something important (love) for less-than-nothing, gives Donald the Junk II and the boys the hourglass.

The boys feel ripped off; it only takes a moment before Donald realizes he's in the same boat, so to speak. Reaching the Junk II, seeing it listing in the water, he reassures himself that at least he's got a better gift than the hourglass. That is, until he is suddenly attacked by the owner of the docks. Owing fees and penalties associated with the hunk of, well, junk, Donald coughs up all his dough.

Fig. 16. The Magic Hourglass, 5:7-8

As with most of the Barks stories involving secret lands and treasures, it takes an elderly man to give them valuable information—a history lesson—that pushes our heroes in the right direction. An elderly junkman, whom the nephews try to sell the hourglass for a whole dime, scoffs at their request and says "and don't try to tell me it's a magic hourglass just because of what's written on the top of it!" (see Fig. 16) The writing, in ancient Arabic (in which the vendor in Duckburg is somehow fluent), reads that when the hourglass keeps perfect time, the owner will "grow richer by the hour!"

The Ducks quickly realize that their fortunes are tied together—with the boat, they can get to Africa to fill that hourglass and make them wealthy (they quickly put two kazillion and two kazillion together to realize that Uncle Scrooge's fortune was founded on this hourglass' magic.) Unfortunately, the boat is in no condition to sail across the Atlantic Ocean (admittedly, it seems too small to cross the sea even in top shape.) Thinking the hourglass might have some residue of good fortune in its red sand, the whole clan close their eyes and begin walking, holding it aloft like a beacon lighting their way through the darkness.

Again, the magic of Disney training came through for Barks here, as the "whatever works" philosophy took hold suddenly. Follow this thread: The Ducks, eyes closed, walk right off the end of the pier and into the drink. Underwater, Donald spies two great white sharks (which tells us for the first time that Duckburg is on the sea.) They race at him, teeth bared. Somehow he dives and they smack their heads against the pier, which knocks them out. So, the ducks tie the groggy sharks to either side of the Junk II, and use them as snarling engines to cross a turbulent sea. (see Plate 7)

I mean, fucking hell. There is an amazing splash panel, one of my favorites, a riotous symphony of movement—Donald sits high atop a chair which is nearly as tall as the mast on the ship, and he's cracking a whip; we see both sharks' faces, with teeth exposed looking very much like the nose of a World War II spitfire with its fangs painted on; one of the kids is halfway up the mast, pointing at the portside shark, the other is at the wheel, while the other checks the rope which binds the starboard shark. This is a turbulent sea, and the Junk II is sliding down the front of the wave, its prow cutting through the sea, water surging onto the deck. And this is in the narration box:

*Father Neptune has seen some strange ships cross his broad oceans, but none stranger than the argosy of the fortune-hunting Ducks!*

But that's it! One magnificent panel, encompassing the whole of their adventure across the sea, and then we cut back to Duckburg, and Scrooge just now figuring out that this hourglass is the secret to his success. We see the worst of his life: trapped in an office while whole rooms full of terrified men sweat profusely, agonizing over the reports that their miserly boss is losing a billion dollars a minute.

And here is another specific detail that sets these stories between the two ducks apart: hyperbole. Donald does some crazy things in his tales, but he is always grounded in our reality. Until we hit the "Brittle Mastery" stories later, we see that Donald's exploits are ridiculous in a screwball comedy way. From sharks guiding a boat, to the search for a Gilded Man, and a lost civilization in the mists of the Andes Mountains—all of these could happen, and in fact they do in our imagination, without tremendous leaps of faith. At one point in "The Magic Hourglass," Scrooge begins weeping and says "I can't go on like this—losing a billion dollars a minute! I'll be broke in 600 years!" Never mind that this joke is stolen from *Citizen Kane* (where Kane jokes that the loss of a million dollars a year on a newspaper will result in the end of his fortune in sixty years, which, in fact, we've already seen occur in flashback), but it also signifies that Scrooge has superhuman wealth. Doing the math, this means his wealth sits at 18,921,600,000,000,000,000 dollars—almost 19 quintillion dollars, in case you're wondering, a sum so grotesque it renders his manic pursuit of the hourglass inhuman. Scrooge's response is to race to the Ducks' home where he demands the hourglass back for a whole dime. Again, an elderly man, clipping the hedge, tells Scrooge that the Ducks are headed to Africa. Now Scrooge is mad: despite the fact that the hourglass does indeed belong to them (thanks to Scrooge's giving it away) he flies to Morocco, where he employs thugs to violently take it from them.

From here, The Magic Hourglass takes on a truly nasty edge, more so than any other Duck comic. This is the bleakness of noir, of Kane, of Stroheim's Greed. I've not found any evidence that Barks was a man captivated by the moving image. By his own admission he barely read books, focusing his attentions on Zane Grey[1] and magazines, and a great fondness for newspaper comics. Like the early Donald in "Maharajah," this early Scrooge is not heroic, but a miser with evil intentions, which only get worse.

Captured by Scrooge's thugs in Morocco, Donald is hauled away and tortured (though the torture involves being tickled into submission… this is, after all, a Disney comic). He confesses that the hourglass is on the boat. But the kids have escaped, into the dark, dangerous port city in Morocco (Casablanca?). Donald's worried—we see knife fights and bottles of booze lying about. But the kids are in disguise, roping Donald and making a hasty retreat to the edge of the Sahara desert.

Suddenly, a man on a camel, brandishing a rifle, appears. When this stranger mentions that Scrooge has a reward on their heads (and yet another instance of Scrooge's brutality—for these offers are no doubt being made to the worst of Morocco's already rampantly criminal underclass), Donald begins putting up his dukes in full cartoon mode. "You won't take us without a fight." This is kind of ridiculous, considering the stranger has a rifle and Donald and the boys have only their fists.

....................
1   Gray was the preeminent writer of westerns in the 20th century.

Fig. 16. The Magic Hourglass, 13:6

But the stranger has an even more bizarre response: To Donald's claim that he won't go without a fight, the stranger says, "That is what I figured: in fact, that's why I came to find you!" Turns out, his caravan has twice been raided by the bandits near the Oasis of No Issa, the only place where the ducks can get their hourglass filled.

Though I love "The Magic Hourglass," appreciating it especially for its strange mix of cruelty, humor, violence, and straight out bat-shit weirdness, clearly Barks just wants to cut to the chase and reach his various climaxes. This meeting, like the crossing of the ocean, takes no time to develop: this dude is so poorly conceived that he doesn't even have a name (Donald calls him "Sheik," but only once). The Sheik needs fighting men, though it appears he has many; as it turns out, he admits that there is no Oasis, but that it must exist because that is the only place these raiders could come from; everyone reaches their destination in a short page, and the Ducks turn out not only to possess an accuracy with a rifle that would make a sniper jealous, but are actually able to give the sheik—who must've made this trek dozens of times—strategies for turning back the bandits.

Sadly, unlike the ocean, the desert did not inflame Barks' artistic chops. The Sahara in "The Magic Hourglass" is nothing more than horizon, barely more than just a slightly wavy line, with blue sky and brown dunes, no swirling sands, no sun, sometimes not even the desert—just Donald or the sheik in close-up against a blank backdrop.

After they beat back the raiders, the Ducks tell the sheik they're leaving the caravan to backtrack the bandits to No Issa. Oddly enough, they don't take any camels, and it is only through the sheik's kindness that they even remember to bring a water bag. This exchange is important, for it will speak to the value of what is truly important, especially in such a harsh climate as the desert, but it also suggests that no one is paying any attention to the dangers around them, least of all Barks, who seemed not to give a hoot about the desert—it's as fundamentally safe as it appears in the Hope/Crosby *Road to Morocco* flick.

Animals and water appear once again, as our men see, in the distance, a lone camel walking with determination. Like the trained monkey in "The Gilded Man," not only does this animal know where it's going, but the Ducks recognize this and use it to their advantage. The camel leads them back to a water hole and then disappears—it turns out the Oasis of No Issa exists in a long tunnel beneath the underground river at the oasis.

Now Barks' imagination became excited again, as we enter a mysterious and beautiful underground palace—replete with gorgeous silks, gold lamps, and large-breasted women in veils, again human (lacking the black button dog nose.) Another nameless sheik fumes because of the failure of the raiders to make a successful raid on the desert caravan. "You dopes were unlucky because you are unsanitary!" he screams, demanding they go bathe in a pile of magical red sand— the same sand that makes the hourglass work its particular miracles.

In a nicely humorous moment, the ducks go to fill the hourglass and accidentally bang one of the fully submerged raiders on the noggin—and, of course, they're instantly captured. Brought before the evil sheik, who threatens to boil them in camel fat, Donald explains that he was only there to fill the hourglass, when the sheik explodes with joy. Here we get the background: the "mighty magician" Hassan Hadda Haircut built the little hourglass centuries earlier. Distracted by the hourglass, the bandits race out of the cave in search of treasure, leaving the Ducks behind.

Back to the surface, we get a nice convergence of the forces moving this story along. Scrooge has relented (in his mind), carrying bags with a billion dollars to buy the hourglass from the nephews. But the raiders attack, taking the hourglass, the money, and scattering Scrooge's men across the wide Sahara.

That is, until one of the raiders holds aloft the hourglass, only to watch in horror as Donald lassos it right out of his hand! Whatever works, whatever works. "With the hourglass in their possession, the Ducks' luck is unbeatable—it almost seems!" Apparently that's true for the ducks, but not the North Africans who possessed it just a couple panels earlier.

Now comes the moral, which isn't much of a surprise, but further reinforces the overall themes we see in Donald's universe. The hourglass only brings them material wealth—a lake of diamonds, a water bag full of gold—but it won't provide what they need most: water. In their haste, the ducks have forgotten this most precious commodity in the raging desert. But the Duck luck outweighs the hourglass. In what I consider a pretty intense panel, content-wise, Scrooge, walking alone (Why doesn't anyone get camels? Is no one worried about walking across the desert, even with water?) encounters the four ducks, collapsed on the sand, tongues out, dying. Then, the nastiness increases—Scrooge walks up with his bulging water bag and his face twists into a rictus of greed, knowing he has them over a barrel. Water for hourglass, no discounts, no deals. (see Plate 8)

The Ducks respond immediately, happily, and then, in the next panel, we see this story's moral summed up nicely: Donald walking, head high, eyes wide, the kids in tight line behind him, the family focused and happy, no longer bickering (as they did in the opening panels of the story), and ruminating on their journey. "Well, our dream of riches may have gone up in smoke, but what does it matter? We're happy!" Donald says.

Remember, it wasn't the search for fortune that pushed them to embark on this journey. At first, the Ducks were trying to get to the bottom of who their uncle loved more, and in the course of this epic fight, involving sharks, cutthroats, torture, gunplay, and treasures won and lost, the family—the Duck family, not Scrooge—is reunited by the end of "The Magic Hourglass." The nephews are no longer at odds with their uncle. They're together now, and their compassion has also returned: When Scrooge offers to trade gold and diamonds for a drink of water, they reject his pleas, until he finally caves in and puts up the hourglass. At this point, Donald decides to give his cruel uncle a drink of water. But with it, Scrooge must keep the hourglass, keep his fortune, and must sail, as they did, all alone across the ocean on the Junk II, with its shark engine.

The story closes with a large and beautifully composed panel, of Uncle Scrooge cursing the ducks and cracking the whip, alone. (see Plate 9) For their efforts in finding the Raiders of No Issa they received a financial reward, which means they can afford a luxury liner that sails in the background of the Junk II. Scrooge is alone, cradling his hourglass; the "winner." The Ducks have some money (presumably the reward will buy them more than just four tickets home), but what they really gained is harmony.

"The Magic Hourglass," despite some of its bizarre structural turns, and an unfascinating look at the Sahara (not to mention fairly lazy rendering of the citizens of Morocco) works in part because of Barks' robust storytelling and the genuine affection for the family of one Donald Duck. Plus, I like this rendering of Uncle Scrooge, as it is the most honest assessment of this bastard's life: lonely, angry, veering into evil to get what he wants. In later Uncle Scrooge comics we'll see an often coldhearted man who, Grinch-like, often gives way to a man who comes to understand kindness and generosity, to which I say bullshit. The Uncle Scrooge of torture, of trying to buy love, of cheating and swindling and browbeating hardworking underlings into submission, is the true Scrooge. Which only makes the Duck family all the more appealing.

Fig. 17. Vacation Time, 4:7

# THE FORGOTTEN MASTERPIECE:
## Vacation Time

Donald Duck has sought his fortune in the jungles of Guiana, the deserts of Morocco, crossed the ocean and, as you'll soon see, will save North America by following the Viking trail up the coast of Newfoundland. In comics not discussed here, he would spelunk deep into the earth, and zoom on rockets to distant asteroids and planets. But Carl Barks' second greatest comic, in my mind (after "The Golden Helmet"), takes Donald just a few hours outside of Duckburg, on a camping trip. Like Buster Keaton, Donald will be initially perceived as a fool only to shed this embarrassing exoskeleton to reveal, in a terrifying and ultimately moving series of events, a hero unlike any in the Barks canon. "Vacation Time" is the name of the story, and it is one of the most incredible comic book tales ever written, brilliantly composed with an array of panels that bend and twist to give a sense of movement and humor, before returning them to 'normal' shape, and thus allowing them to communicate the gravity of the scene within their borders. "Vacation Time" is Carl Barks' *General*, Donald's best performance, and perhaps the best kept secret in comics.

I don't know what happened to Barks to make him lose his mind on this particular story, but I'm glad that he did. Barks pulled out all the stops in making this as hilarious as any of the slapsticks from cinema's silent era (when they were at their best), but this is slapstick of the finest construction, a series of hilarious events that build to a crescendo that suddenly becomes devastatingly tragic.

Barks' plots are tight and economical, much like the stories that Howard Hawks liked to tell, of groups of men who might bicker with one another, but who ultimately trust and rely upon each other to get a job done. Working at Disney seemed to imprint on the comics-auteur an ability to make these thirty-plus page stories like a master. Barks' plots did't meander as Hawks' often did, but like Hawks' they eschewed backstory. The brilliance of Donald Duck stories is that Barks knew that the lack of continuity freed him to make Donald slip into any role. We know Donald, right? Well, no—we actually don't know Donald's skills in any particular story, not at all. In "The Gilded Man," we're not aware that he's able to instantly gaze upon a stamp and determine its value, something we learn in the present moment in that particular story. Like Hawks' great works (and if you're unfamiliar, you really need to see *Only Angels Have Wings*, *His Girl Friday*, *The Big Sleep*, *Red River*, *Rio Bravo*, among others), character is revealed to us, in the moment. Barks understood that we don't need to learn the hows and whys that brought Donald to pick up stamp collecting. He just does and he just is.

So it is in "Vacation Time"—we will come to see that Donald is a master camper, someone who knows exactly how to behave as a model citizen in a National Park, and a person who, as it turns out, can act cool and collected even as a wildfire of epic proportions bears down upon them. Who knew?

"Vacation Time" avoids many of the usual (and effective) plot points one sees in other Barks comics: gone is the lowly worker, bored and seeking adventure; gone is the drive for money; gone is the old man or animal that reveals the path to adventure. In a sense, "Vacation Time" is not an adventure—like Keaton's *The General*, it is a story of a guy who just wants to do his job (or in this case, take a camping trip), but has a series of mishaps that are funny, until he is faced with a treacherous situation that exposes his brilliance and resolve.

I've stated before that perhaps my favorite aspect to Donald Duck is this sense that he's an actor in a series of different stories, the "paper movies," highlighting his different skills and his comic chops. Yes, Donald often fails, but here his failures are small, albeit hilarious, while his heroics are extreme, all the while he remains fully in character. I mention Keaton a few times because Donald Duck's character, in his own comics (as opposed to the Scrooge comics,) has similar attributes. Keaton's character, which changed throughout his films, nonetheless had characteristics that remained the same throughout his movies: he was resourceful, often unlucky (but resigned to that fate with the calm of a Buddhist), prone to fucking things up but wriggling free from these errors. If "Vacation Time" had been a movie, I can imagine it as a Buster Keaton film.

The stage is set in a remarkable, full-page splash panel, in which Donald and the boys, driving reliable old "313," their nifty red jalopy, look poised at the edge of disaster. Really, the perspective here is something you couldn't see in real life, unless this part of the world was bent and twisted in such a way as to be able to see from various angles, Escher-like.

First of all, the car. I've always loved Donald's cozy little red convertible: a flivver with gray balloon-y wheels, bright red, a single seat in front. This seat is wide enough for Donald and one other duck-sized person, or a big jerk (like the villain of this story) who fills the entire seat. In lieu of a trunk, there's a rumble seat where the boys sit. We see green canvas tents and sleeping bags strapped snakelike over the fender and across the doors, and old-style leather suitcases with metal edges roped to the hood. The license plate (which you can't see here) always reads "313." This is a kid's car, or really, a child's dream car, and you imagine it racing along, airborne at times, light enough to be picked up by a large bloke. I'll take this thing over the Batmobile any day.

The opening panel is a whirl of action. Donald and the boys are slightly airborne in old 313, indicating speed. Our man's taking a curve fast, wide-eyed and smiling, almost tumbling over the side of the road and off into a rushing waterfall that ends below in a whirlpool (with vultures circling overhead.) A snarling mountain lion, as big as the car, is poised to leap from a branch in the upper left, while a raging bear pursues the car in the upper right. In his eagerness to get out of the city, Donald's racing so fast that he fails to notice he's almost bouncing the boys out of the back—Huey reaches out for Donald, while Dewey hangs on for dear life, clutching Louie, who has just fallen off the rear and almost into the jaws of the bear.

"Ah! Vacation time! The one season of the year when we can get away from the dangers of city living!" Donald says with a happy smile on his face, oblivious to the many threats on this mountain road.

From here on out we will get the standard eight panel per page layout (with some variations), but the panels, as if on some sort of laughing gas, will bend and point and make room for a world which is meant to be as elastic as salt-water taffy. The joke of the first giant panel— that this treacherous world is perceived as safer than the big city of Duckburg—is repeated through the next two pages, with Donald as usual getting everyone lost.

The difference here, and one that we'll see played out later, is that "Vacation Time" is definitely Donald's terrain—the boys will help, will laugh at their uncle, but it is Donald who is in charge, and it is he who saves them. He is oblivious to danger here, but when he does see it, he reacts bravely.

After that first joke, Barks' comic timing kicks in beautifully, filling each panel with lovely detail, as the family climbs the mountains heading to the National Park where they'll camp. "Peaceful country roads! No trucks roaring at you from blind cross streets!" he says as a mountain locomotive bears down on them. "No traffic jams! No

noise!" he observes as they squeeze across a mountain bridge that
is jam packed with sheep. A hay truck will nearly push them into a
ditch while Donald complains about city road hogs, and later, when
he repairs an already well-patched inner tube, he wonders aloud how
he'd survive if he had to fix the flat on the corner of Wilshire and
Vermont (back in Duckburg, one presumes.) As he says this, two
wolves and a coiling rattlesnake appear ready to strike, yet only the
nephews are sweating.

Visually, the page is split into two halves, each half taking the clan
deeper into the wilderness. The "editing" here is spot-on: just as a
motion picture moves you along with the removal of banal information
between action shots, so, too, does Barks carry these Ducks up the
mountain pass swiftly, for maximum comic effect. In each half of page
two, which is made up of seven total panels, the panels bend inward,
bringing the eye, as in the first large page, into distinct focal points,
a sort of cone that the Ducks strive to move toward as they try and
reach their destination. The top four panels point inward, the little car
is always pointing in the direction in which the panel is bent, leading
them toward that same center, which heads to their destination.
Deeper and deeper into this friendly abyss we'll go.

This is a fish out of its urban water—Donald is oblivious, of course, to
the dangers of the wild, the beasts and the uneven roads. Though who
hasn't been a passenger in a car on a mountain road and felt as though
the driver didn't know what they were doing? Presumably Donald
can see the road in front of him, even if he can't see the screaming
eagle bearing down on them in the large panel in the bottom half of
page two. This one is another favorite, and indicates the almost magic
nature of the 313 auto: Donald's at the wheel on a steep incline, so
steep that one boy pushes it at the bumper, another pushes at the long
end of a stick (which makes no sense, insofar as physics is concerned,
but who cares), and another nephew pulls the car up with a rope, all
the while that golden eagle seems determined to pluck their smiling

uncle from the cockpit of the car.

Finally on leveler ground, the ducks reach a fork in the road, whose sign is shot to pieces, and Donald has to make a decision which direction to go—of course, he makes the wrong one and, of course, he makes bold claims that he knows exactly where they're going as he "[has] a sixth sense—like a homing pigeon, you know!" One of my favorite subtle jokes sees Huey, out of the car and with a magnifying glass looking at the road, saying "Unca Donald, this road is getting awfully dim!" To determine they're on the wrong road, one of the kids had to climb out and use a magnifying glass? No reason, except that it's funny.

In spite of the great lengths Barks has gone through to show them climbing into vast mountain wilderness, the world down this fork flattens into a hillbilly wasteland, where we get one panel of perhaps my favorite joke (and one I wouldn't have understood as a child—in fact, I didn't discover this comic until I was an adult): two bearded Hillbillies, rifles drawn, stare down at the Ducks, whose path is blocked by a pig. "Revenoors!" the one cries. "An' a-ridin' an ottymobile! Fust one I ever seed!" the other notes, taking aim. The ducks continue on until they reach a stone marker indicating that this is the road back to Duckburg.

Nothing comes of this detour, and in fact these jokes serve dual purposes: first and foremost they work, and make us laugh, but they also communicate that we have not actually entered the boundaries within which this story will settle. The crazy moonshiners, the train, the wildlife run amok... this is not a legitimate danger zone, it is a land of comic possibilities, as indicated by the fact that not only does Donald not act heroically, but the nephews cower, too. Their cowering—as Donald nearly kills them—communicates to us to just enjoy the ride. This is the easy part: the terrors that Donald blindly gropes by in order to get to his natural paradise... and real danger.

And the paradise in this case is what appears to be a National Forest in, as Donald states earlier, the fictional Eagleclaw Mountains. On page four, the jokes suddenly cease, as do our elastic panels (albeit just for this page for now.) Here, our hero pays a visit to the ranger station, in order to get a fire permit and instructions. "We want this scenery to still be here when we leave!" Now nature is in harmony with the Ducks: squirrels and chipmunks come right up to their vehicle and even stand on the Ducks' heads. The ranger, a tall, upright man with perfectly creased pants, is delighted at Donald's preparation—the ranger feels assured that the Ducks are going to follow the rules and leave nature as it was.

As they drive on to their campsite, the streams are pristine, burbling, no longer threatening whirlpools that can suck them to their deaths. Gone are the fierce creatures, the crazy roads and narrow, crumbling bridges, the snarling hillbillies. At the campsite, Donald orders his nephews about, who valiantly (and judging from

Fig. 18. Vacation Time, 5:5

their faces, exhaustively) clear away pine needles and haul rocks to make the perfect, fire-safe campsite. This is all Donald's work in terms of its organization, which the nephews recognize. This is an orderly campsite, functional and, above all, safe, and we can almost smell the wood smoke and the canvas tent, warmed by the sun. (see Fig. 18) We shall soon see the result of a disorderly campsite.

What occurs next becomes a strange hybrid of Donald Duck meets Bambi meets Keaton. For eighteen crazy pages, Donald's a hot-tempered camera hound, trying desperately to capture a majestic buck on film. Along the way, the kids end up cavorting with nature themselves, surrounded by little fawns, does and rabbits—nature in perfect harmony. On this jaunt, Donald collides with a nameless, cigarette smoking bully, whom our hero chides (and fistfights) because the bully is a terrible camper, and a careless one at that.

This is where Donald the comic actor really shines. Like, say, Laurel and Hardy or Abbot and Costello being dumped into a wilderness setting, we settle in to watch our man try his best to relax and fail from almost the first step. We know, without question, that he is going to meet comic disaster. Waking at dawn, racing to the mountain stream and shouting at his sleepy nephews to get coffee on the fire, Donald tries to hook some breakfast. Right away he gets a strike—his hook gets caught on the rack of a giant buck, and after getting rammed by the noble beast, Donald's gears begin to whir: he can make a pot of money taking a stunning photo of the animal (we see our hero dreaming of a framed photo of the deer with a blue ribbon slapped on it, and dollar signs floating above his head). (see Plate 10) The machine of the joke is apparent, but again, the joy is watching it play itself out. We know that Donald will not get his shot. We know there will be a series of ever increasing defeats, and we wait with eagerness for them to unfold.

But before embarking on the fun, Barks understands that he also needs to assert his plot at some point. Racing back for his camera, Donald is himself hooked by another fisherman, a lumbering,

Marlboro-smoking, Brooklyn-accented rummy who insults Donald and also tosses a still-burning match into high grass. When Donald leaps to put the match out, and chides the jerk, the latter responds by calling our man a "scared old grandma" and rubbing Donald's face in the wet grass. So Donald rolls up his sleeves and sets about to teach the firebug a lesson, and of course gets the crap beat out of him.

Freed from the clutches of the smoker, Donald grabs his trusty camera and chases the deer, runs into bears, has a shot but has no film in his camera, gets tossed into a stream and eventually head-butted by the buck, which he continually fails to photograph.

Before we move on to the climax, you have to wonder about Barks' motivation. As mentioned, Barks was not a traveler, as finances (and probably his own lack of ambition) kept him homebound. While he was creating "Vacation Time" his second marriage was in collapse, and he was preparing himself to abandon any thoughts of making a fortune, looking forward to grinding out a living instead. His first marriage, which resulted in two children, was long over, and this one, to a raging alcoholic, was coming to a nasty close. Where his other comics took Donald to South America, India, or the Bering Sea, and therefore relied on his imagination and the stunning work of *National Geographic* and the staff of the *Encyclopedia Britannica*, Vacation Time, which is one of his most richly detailed works, might in fact stem from a welcome retreat from the horrors of home life.

Was Barks a man who could once in awhile escape from work and a lousy home life to the mountains, hit the camping trail for a bit, and relax? Was Donald's "getting back to nature" the most palatable escape that Barks was capable of, both in terms of his time and his finances?

Looking over "Vacation Time," one is filled with a sense of peace and calm, despite the manic pace of the shenanigans that Donald and the boys are up to.

Barks once described himself as being like a stage director, but here we really see that his Donald Duck comics are the perfect "paper movies"—the world of Carl Barks is too great to be confined to a "stage." His "direction" here is faultless, as page after page revels in a series of bent panels, each one with its close-up, medium-, or long distance shots to achieve maximum effect. Consider page 15, where we see the climax of a chase between Donald and the elusive buck. The nephews have flushed the deer toward a boulder upon which Donald hopes to achieve a rather noble shot. However, a bear has snuck up behind him, unthreatening, wearing a look of dumb curiosity. On the next page, the top four panels are again bent in such a way as to point inward toward one focal point. In the upper left, the trapezoid shows Donald about ready to snap a photo when the bear snatches the camera from his hand. The next panels in the top half are all five sided polygons, bending toward a center of all the action. The bottom half is divided by a page-wide panel that narrows to the left (the direction you're reading), and the bottom two panels slant upwards. The sequence goes as follows:

1.) Donald is about to snap a picture but the bear, whose chest and arm are all we see, snatch the camera from him.

2.) Donald turns, infuriated, in full close up, shouting "Hey! What's the big idea?"

3.) The next panel, extremely narrow like a tower, sees Donald racing up the rock, hat flying off, blubbering "A b-b-b-b-b-bear!"

4.) then, the collision: Donald and Buck meet, head on, in the largest panel on the top half, stars and the word SPLAT!

5.) Next page-wide panel has the bear in the wider half, actually taking the picture with a "Click!", bewildered, while the deer stands, legs akimbo, Donald underneath, both loopy from the collision and looking like a couple of drunken pals after a bender;

6.) Next, the bear is leaping away, reacting to the click of the camera, and leaving it behind.

7.) And then we conclude with Donald, gazing past us, head in hands, a black "CENSORED" bar in his word balloon, while the buck dances away from us, tail in the air, ass toward the reader (and our hero). (see Plate 11)


This description doesn't do justice to the speed with which Barks moved this story along. Slapstick requires swift movement, it requires a precise editor who maximizes each image for its full comic effect, and we get that here. We even get Donald breaking the fourth wall, as he gets exasperated to the point of seeking understanding directly from the reader. (see Fig. 19)

After fifteen pages of this slapstick, cavorting through this magnificent forest (and I have to say that these moments are not only funny but totally relaxing—Barks has captured this National Forest beautifully) we begin to get indications of trouble. As Donald pursues the buck, finally about to capture a perfect pose, he smells smoke. And here the story turns into one of danger, a more realistic and threatening problem than in any of the Duck comics. In fact, this shared concern for the smoke results in a subtle suggestion of harmony: when Donald smells it, he actually climbs on top of the deer he's been chasing for a better look.

"Vacation Time," up to this point a straightforward comedy, becomes fraught with

Fig. 19. Vacation Time, 12:3

Fig. 20. Vacation Time, 25:5

danger, as well as poignant despair. The panels straighten out in response to our sudden concern. As the ducks race to their site in an attempt to get to their car and thus escape with their lives, they move against a vast tide of animals plowing in the opposite direction, panicked from the approaching inferno. Upon arrival, they find the jalopy gone—the villain of this story has stolen it. In one of the most moving panels of Barks' whole oeuvre, we see a "normal" rectangular panel, the left half forest, the right half flames that tower nearly twice as high, and these three word balloons:

*We – Are – Doomed!* (see Fig. 20)

We then see the ducks crouched, the upper three-quarters of the next two panels gray with smoke, one of the nephews desperately wondering if they should hide in a stream ("and get boiled like eggs?" the other complains).

But it is here that we see Donald the adult take over. "Wait! Stay together! I'll think of something!" Clearly, the young Ducks are frightened, confused, but Donald is thinking clearly. In the next scene, we see a panorama of the forest, ringed by fire. Someone, Donald or one of the boys, says "The fire is circling us along the ridges! There is no way out!" But in the next panel Donald is decisive, urging his nephews to grab shovels and canteens. He will be the one to save the day, to take charge.

Here, Barks cuts away to the villain, tucked behind the wheel of the little red convertible, safe on a high mountain road. He literally kicks the car over the cliff so as not to be caught with it.

There's a great story about Buster Keaton's *The Navigator*, the silent film classic that takes place on a deserted ship. At one point, Buster is underwater, while the heroine of the film is being attacked by cannibals. Keaton originally shot an involved (and expensive) scene with him directing, like a traffic cop in a diving bell, schools of fish that go swimming by—audiences hated it, because they were too busy being freaked out by the attack on the girl above water to care about this silly moment undersea. Keaton chopped it out to keep the story intact.

Barks could not cut away and leave us worrying about the Ducks, especially since he was so effective in showing that, for once, these guys are in extreme trouble. In other comics, Donald has been on the verge of being sacrificed by a gilded man, fed to lions, sank in a ship, gunned down… but this forest fire is almost too real. In other instances, we just assume the boys will get him out of every jam, and they always do—here, the boys are conceding death, gripping their uncle, readying for the worst. But we're reassured, because we know, from the panel in which he demands they bring a canteen and shovels, that he has a plan.

The gravity of their situation is reinforced next with some of Barks' best drawing, as we see scores of rangers racing with fire trucks, parachuting down into the fire, a helicopter hovering overhead, being pushed back by a mountain-sized cloud of ash, and the pilot exclaiming "Nobody can escape with their lives!" Even the bully, standing with his back to us, staring at a wall of fire, gloats that there will be no witnesses to his carelessness. If we didn't know that this scene is hopeless, we certainly do now.

Barks took us back to the Ducks, whose escape is strange to say the least, yet totally believable. Emerging into an open field, the towering fire at their heels, Donald orders the nephews to dig little trenches— graves essentially. Soaking their jackets with water, he lays each on the faces of his nephews, and hands them shovels. In a haunting panel, we see one of the nephews, face hidden beneath the coat, laying backward in this grave, scared, saying "You can't bury us! We'll suffocate!" Donald, now sporting a tank top (his jacket is off, soaked with water), responds testily, "Shut up and put this shovel blade over your head!" Walking by the three mounds that are his nephews, he digs little air holes for them, until finally burying himself as best he can just moments before the panel is engulfed in flame.

We cut momentarily to the ranger's office, where we find the villain of this piece, chain- smoking and trying to lay the blame for the fire on the Ducks. He is infuriating, and our only saving grace is that the chief ranger seems surprised that the Ducks would have committed such a grievous error, all the while looking sideways at the smoke from this bum's cig. Doing this also allows us to realize that the fire's out, for Barks' has taken us away from the Ducks because we know their gambit worked. It gives us just enough tension, but also reflects our confidence (and obviously Barks') in his hero.

Sure enough, they survived, and come out of their trenches. In a heartbreaking contrast to the beauty he had created in the joyous earlier pages, Barks shows us nothing but destruction—the whole forest, in a haunting splash panel, burned to brown and black, charred trunks and wisps of smoke. (see Plate 12) As they wander through this wasteland, past the once blue stream now brown with ash and mud, they seem strangely serene, happy, perhaps, to be alive.

If I have a criticism of "Vacation Time," it's that the ending is too pat for my taste—they return to the ranger station, where the bully is shocked to see them alive. A confrontation ensues, and then it turns out one of the boys has Donald's camera which, we discover, contains a shot of Donald arguing with the bully and showing his dangerous campground, enough to… what? Convict him? What happens to a guy that starts a forest fire?

Vindicated, the ranger tells the boys that they can camp anywhere in the forest, and that the rangers will furnish their whole outfit (presumably their stuff's been torched.) For good measure (and at the whispered plea of one of the kids), the rangers confiscate Donald's camera, so that the trip will continue in peace. Our last panels show them having the time of their lives, sleeping, playing, and not taking any pictures. Great—except that we were treated, quite realistically, to the fact that damn near all the campground burned right down to the ground, and we're back to blue streams and trees and even the deer posing for a picture Donald isn't allowed to take. My assumption is that this is a huge park, and this is simply a part that didn't burn, but still.

"Vacation Time" is moving because, though I love the other stories here, this one seems both grounded in the real world (forest fires, rangers) and in the unreal (the mad race to get that damn picture). It is one of Barks' few domestic stories (except for the work tales I discuss in the last essay), and I like that the real world pushes Donald into heroics that transcend virtually any that he's faced before, if only because, while it's true that he kind-of literally saves the whole of North America from enslavement, that story ("The Golden Helmet") is pure fantasy. "Vacation Time" is, in a sense, the story of a man who simply wanted to take a vacation, who respects nature, respects the rules of our National Parks, and then, when disaster strikes, risks his life and coolly saves his children from death. The kids are kids, and the adult here is an adult, a model citizen, and, dare I say, a real hero.

Fig. 21. The Golden Helmet, 22:6

# ONE HELMET TO RULE THEM ALL:
## *The Golden Helmet*

Carl Barks consistently referred to "Lost in the Andes" as his finest work, but I would counter with "The Golden Helmet." "Helmet," with its almost zen-like appraisal of a peaceful life, its condemnation of greed and avarice (not to mention lawyers), a story that has humor but not too much, that actually takes itself somewhat seriously, is his finest effort, at the very least in terms of writing (though the art is brilliant as usual). Barks' claimed that the gags in "Andes" were executed perfectly, the repeating jokes of the gum bubbles and the square eggs, etc., and this is true—but "Helmet," whose themes run smoothly through this story, is less reliant on knee-slapping gags. "The Golden Helmet" isn't just a story of adventure, a story of humor, or even bravery (though those traits exist here.) "The Golden Helmet" is Barks' most somber effort, a story of evil, the evil that lurks in everyone. Even children.

Barks' visual style in "The Golden Helmet" seems to also suggest that we're in for a more sobering ride. Gone are the crazy splash panels of "Vacation Time" (or any of the other stories mentioned here, almost all of which have a bent panel or two at least). For the opening scene, as with the rest of this tale, there will be not one skewed panel. Splash panels vanish until twelve pages in, and even then there will be only four of them.

In fact, the opening scene, is one of stasis, boredom. (see Fig. 22) Contrast the narration with the opening of "Lost in the Andes." Both feature Donald working at a museum: in the latter, Barks wrote, "It is morning of a day destined to live long in history! At the Museum of Natural Science the third assistant janitor is giving orders to the fourth assistant janitor!" This joke just brims with energy. Donald has a huge smile on his face, even as he holds a feather duster.

Here, the narration box simply reads, "Donald is the assistant guard in the Museum at Duckburg!" A guard strikes me as a more intriguing position than janitor, and yet in "The Golden Helmet," Donald leans against a sculpture of a strange looking "prehistoric cow" (as the placard reads), his eyes are almost closed, and he's bored beyond belief. Donald's opening line? "Ho hum!" The Museum doesn't even have a name—the "Museum at Duckburg?"—and gone is the joke about multiple assistants, even though he's an assistant guard.

A Viking ship will play a large part in this tale, as Barks foreshadowed his plot points as usual—there's a big Viking ship in the background, with a large placard describing the thing. Banality wins out: "Old Viking Ship" (there's no more descriptive term than that?) And this: "This ancient hulk was dug up in Herring, Norway, where it was buried by the Vikings about 920 A.D." "Hulk" suggests that this ship is merely junk, and the bland sentence communicates simply the most rote facts, and even those aren't all that interesting.

In this opening page, Donald wanders the museum (as a guard must do), alternating between yawning and bemoaning his fate, a fate of having nothing to do. The museum offers a collection of history's detritus: the Headless Horseman's toupee, Lady Godiva's laundry bag, and, perhaps most telling, a morose statue with a long face, titled "Joy." At the close of the first page, and over the next few, Donald has circled back to the Viking ship, where he muses over how soft modern man has become. So here the theme asserts itself: the boredom of

Fig. 22. The Golden Helmet, 2:2

modern man. The vessels and castoffs of history's bravest people are trapped in these four walls and behind glass, while we simply wander about, dazed, gazing upon them. At this point, a fat, myopic man with Coke-bottle glasses asks where to find the butterfly collection, leaving Donald shaking his head. And when an effete fellow with large eyelashes says, "Mister Guard, where is the lace and tatting collection?" Donald cannot help but actually climb aboard the "hulk" and pretend, in his words, that he is a "he-man."

It is while he's playing this game of the imagination that Donald stumbles across the villain of the piece, Azure Blue, a craggy, goatee'd sourpuss who's breaking the ship apart looking for a map. Donald shoos him away and then, of course, discovers the map that will transport him from Duckburg to the high seas.

This is quite a find. No mere treasure map, it is, instead, a "log of that old Viking ship!", as the museum's curator points out. The curator is a friendly soul, balding, bushy beard, but oddly enough he will never have a name other than "The Curator". The scene that follows is reminiscent of the opening (though not the prologue) of *Raiders of the Lost Ark*: in The Curator's office, we learn that the map reveals that the ship was helmed by one Olaf the Blue, and that in the year 901 landed on the coast of North America, "years before Eric the Red!" (The man who truly "discovered" America.) To prove that he landed on the shore of North America, Olaf buried the eponymous helmet, and the map points to exactly where this thing is located. Excited that the Duckburg Museum has proof of exactly who discovered America, the Curator spins Donald around, happily shouting, "You'll be famous! The museum will be famous!"

Ready to dispatch an expedition to retrieve the prize, the Curator is suddenly interrupted by Azure Blue and his lawyer, Sharky, who spouts a weird Latinate legalbabble. They demand the map, claiming that Blue is the descendant of the original Olaf, and that by owning said helmet Azure will, in fact, become the King of North America.

Barks concocted a wonderful historical mini-backstory, suggesting that during the time of Charlemagne the rulers of the world agreed that whomever discovers a new land shall own it, unless he claims it for his king. Olaf claimed it for himself, so now it goes to his distant relative, Azure Blue. "How can you prove he is Olaf's nearest of kin?" The Curator shouts, to which Sharky replies, "Flickus, Flackus, Fumdeedledum!", and then: "Which is legal language for, 'How can you prove that he isn't?'" And with that, they grab the map, and head out the door to retrieve the Golden Helmet.

What's interesting is that this is essentially an adventure of attitudes. Whereas, say, in *Raiders*, Indy is out for adventure, but he's also going to help stop a menace that is physical—the Nazis will use the Ark of the Covenant to literally destroy other, freedom-loving armies. With the Ark, they could (had their faces not been melted off and heads exploded) ruled the world against everyone's will. Here, this is a threat of perception: if Azure Blue gets the helmet, he will own North America, but his control over the continent depends solely on whether the population as a whole actually believes him to be so. It depends on armies of lawyers and politicians, each one, we imagine, angling for whatever advantage they can get from Blue. Such is the power of this "law" that it will even dissolve boundaries—notice that the owner of the Golden Helmet is not king of America or Canada, but North America.

This is what modern man has come to: if someone says they're the king of North America, we won't fight, but merely hope that politicians and lawyers can get us out of this mess.

Even before we can get this story rolling, we need to see the worst of people, this time in the kids. Donald races home to find his nephews stupidly shooting marbles in the living room, bored, eyes half closed, making one wonder if kids back then were as challenged to get out and about as they are today. So ignorant of geography that one of them asks if Labrador is a coat, Donald runs headlong into a wall out of exasperation. But soon they're on their way, taking an all-night flight to Labrador (with a nifty fold out queen-sized bed in it—man, travel was awesome back then).

The chase is on. And we notice that the sea excited Barks more than any other landscape. Inspired by the richly detailed newspaper comic strip *Prince Valiant*, Barks played not only with the breathtaking visuals

Fig. 23. The Golden Helmet, 12:3

of a turbulent sea, but also with a rocky coastline that is as inhospitable as Mars. This is a bleak, unforgiving world that encompasses this chase, and Blue is ready for it, with his yacht, filled with reporters (to verify his finding the helmet), and a warship (strangely numbered '313,' same as Donald's jalopy) for protection. On the other hand, Donald will give chase in a smaller boat, tossed about by the waves. "It isn't speed that's going to win this race—it's ruggedness!" he says, as a cold spray blasts him at the wheel of his boat. (see Fig. 23)

Again, Barks revealed Donald's impressive skills through action: he's adept with a sextant and compass, knowing exactly where he's going with both. Like the fire scenes in "Vacation Time," he presses forwards, even as scores of puffins sail by in the opposite direction, away from an impending storm. Eventually, things get so rough even the destroyer turns around, and Azure's ship is crashed upon an iceberg.

We know this because Donald spies the crew of Blue's ship, and its passengers, in lifeboats heading back south. And he is not the least bit interested in seeing if he can help, or even radioing for help, and in fact the boys dance a little jig, celebrating their victory. The race for this helmet has already stripped our heroes of their humanity.

Of course, it cannot be this simple, as the luck of Azure Blue demands that, in a thick fog, he accidentally encounters the ducks and steals their boat, leaving them to survive in a life raft themselves. But they're equally fortunate: discovering the wreckage of Azure's boat, which includes a sail, they're able to jerry-rig a mast and shoot across the sea and up the coast just like Vikings, and in hot pursuit.

Azure reaches the coast first, the location of the helmet, and yet cannot find it, thus prompting Sharky, his lawyer to sneer that Azure should "sue somebody—anybody." This particular comic was written in late 1951 or early 1952, during or just after the time when Barks was involved in an awful divorce from his alcoholic second wife. Lawyers no doubt left a bitter taste in his mouth, and thus Sharky provides

Fig. 24. The Golden Helmet, 19:4

a constantly negative (and at times tiresome) dialogue, suggesting, again and again, that Azure can sue for every setback life sends him. (see Fig. 24)

But Sharky's important, at least in the way that this odd story is constructed: Azure can only make his claim through the power of law, which Barks seemed to believe was eminently pliable, provided you had a good lawyer. Without Sharky, this adventure loses its power, a power that becomes seriously warped as the story progresses.

Donald is able to withstand the worst the sea has to offer, and though the kids endure this as well, they do so with a lot of complaining. Up and down the headland they go, vainly seeking the cross-marked spot, to no avail. Finally, Azure and Sharky literally crash into Donald and the boys yet again, this time ramming their boat and sinking them offshore.

But this helps our heroes. Washed ashore, one of the kids realizes that the cross-shaped headland would in fact erode over time— and it turns out they're standing right by the mound that contains the Golden Helmet. (And ensconced beneath a puffin's nest—when Donald goes to retrieve it, he gets a "golden helmet" of smashed eggs on his head. Again, eggs!)

Looking through binoculars, Blue sees that Donald has the helmet, and in the one mediocre plot twist, steals it back from Donald by... sneaking up and taking it from him. After Blue sneers and proclaims victory, as they march toward his boat (where the Ducks are to become his slaves), the Curator drops a stone on Blue's head, and takes the Helmet yet again. With the evil prize safely in his possession, the Curator demands they board the ship and sail into deep waters, where he can toss the thing into the ocean.

And now comes the dark heart of "The Golden Helmet." As they sail deeper and deeper into the Atlantic, which becomes as bleak and depressing as the desert in "The Magic Hourglass," the backgrounds become sparse, languid. The seas have waves, but the ship moves in a straight, flat line across each panel. Gone is adventure, gone is the turbulence (and beauty) of the Atlantic, and what remains is pure avarice.

For the Curator, on Sharky's advice, decides to keep the Golden Helmet. Since Sharky has proven that anyone can be Olaf the Blue's kin, the Curator has as much right to be the owner of North America as Azure Blue, or anyone else for that matter. "Everybody will have to go to a museum twice a day!" he proclaims, and then proceeds to list off all the museum-friendly things that will occupy the lives of North Americans under his rule.

But the Curator is exhausted. He collapses, and Donald grabs the Helmet. Midway to tossing it into the sea, Donald suddenly has a vivid image of himself, clad in ermine, sitting atop a gold throne that reads KING of North America. Sharky leans in, whispering, and tells our man that a good lawyer can finagle the legal angle.

Donald's full of life now, shouting, "I won't take a thing away from them!" as the Helmet, which he's wearing, comes down over his eyes. When Sharky inquires about what Donald expects to possess, he sneers that he's going to force people to wear meters on their chests and pay him for the very air we breathe. (see Fig. 25)

Fig. 25. The Golden Helmet, 28:1

Leave it to Donald to take this to its farthest point, even growing paranoid and depositing everyone—including his nephews—on an iceberg when he thinks they're trying to steal back the Helmet. But one of the kids sneaks the compass from Donald, leaving him, on a cloudy day, unable to read the stars to determine where he's sailing.

After a polar bear lands on Donald's ship, devouring all their supplies (Sharky has joined him, of course), the Helmet and its power do little to feed either of them (much like the conclusion of "The Magic Hourglass"). Suddenly, through the fog we see a Viking ship—Huey, Dewey and Louie took an axe and shaped the iceberg like the old hulk in the museum (and well done, boys).

Donald is so happy to see his nephews that he renounces ownership, which of course makes Sharky grab the Helmet and proclaim himself owner, but by now everyone's tired of the joke (and besides Donald was the best, evilest owner, anyway.) One of the boys grabs a fish and hurls it in Sharky's face. The Golden Helmet flies from his hand and down, down into the depths, never to be seen again.

So we come around full circle. Donald's had his adventure, even had a close up look at the worst instincts in his own breast, and is back to work at the museum. The laywer is back to his job, we presume, the Curator back curating. "That rugged life had its points—but I don't know—" Donald says, staring again at the Viking ship. His ruminations are interrupted by another effete gentlemen, with giant eyelashes and weird pursed lips, who asks where to find the embroidered lampshades. As Donald begins to give directions, he gives up, choosing instead to take the man there. "Darned if I ain't interested in embroidered lampshades, myself!"

What is the message here? Was it simply to tell people not to question their peaceful lives? The opening scenes of "The Golden Helmet" suggest a world of total banality, of boredom. But by its end the notion that the adventurous life is worth living—even if it's not financially rewarding—has vanished, with the final panels, suggesting that this life, this comfortable life in America, is worth living, dull though it may be. Barks was no doubt sick of lawyers, but perhaps "The Golden Helmet" is a note to himself, a suggestion to give up any dreams of wealth, to celebrate simply working as a Disney artist with its meager pay. Is this Zen-like resignation to the nature of our prosperous banality, or Barks giving up on life? I don't know, but I do love the bitter aftertaste of "The Golden Helmet," which remains, to me, a startling concoction even by Barks' often dark standards.

Fig. 26. Spare That Hair, 1:4

## WORKING MAN:
### *Land of the Totem Poles, No Such Varmint, and the Work Stories*

Everyone works, for the most part. Your parents worked, and maybe even as a child you held down a job delivering newspapers or raking the yard for your allowance or maybe even selling magazine subscriptions or Grit door-to-door. When you hit high school perhaps you slung burgers at McDonald's or mowed lawns or sold pot. In any case, you worked, and did so with varying degrees of success, just like everyone.

If you're reading this book, the chances are pretty good that you're not a millionaire, not a wealthy CEO, but someone who schleps through each day, earning your bread. In his stories, Donald often works his tail off, in a variety of different positions, and here we see actor and creator in perfect synch with one another. Barks worked, from the time he dropped out of high school at age 15 to help his pop out with their farm, and on through retirement, as he painted Duck portraits (with Disney's permission) to supplement his meager income in his dotage. With his hero, Barks captured, with amazing thoroughness, the essence of work—its lows and its highs—better than anyone, in part because he experienced it firsthand, and never stopped experiencing the rigors of day labor. Even as a writer for Western Publishing, churning out the great Duck stories, Barks was fiddling around with chicken farms. His failures informed his hero. And in the final analysis, as you'll see here, Donald is better for his work, better for his labors, even when he fails. And he fails often—until he succeeds.

*The Bhagavad Gita* states, "Work alone is your privilege, never the fruits thereof. Never let the fruits of action be your motive; and never cease to work... Be not affected by success or failure." This very Eastern approach to labor certainly smacks headlong into America's very capitalist approach to working hard and attaining a fortune. As I've stated before, and have shown in two of these comics—"Luck of the North" and "The Gilded Man"—Donald does emerge rich, though in both cases what we had was essentially a treasure hunt existing outside the realm of work. Though both of those stories involved working hard for the treasures involved, neither was about an actual job. (In fact, we may wonder what exactly Donald does that he can take time off for his pursuits.)

"Land of the Totem Poles" shows Donald hard at work as a salesman, and it's a fun and utterly ridiculous story, made wonderful by Barks' insane attention to detail. We open in Duckburg, a city that seems gripped by a happy indolence. A squirrel is perched on Donald's toes as he reads the paper on a park bench, while behind him is a statue of a fat guy in swim trunks hosing himself off. Our hero's intrigued by an ad: "Wanted: super salesmen to sell high-priced gizmo!... huge commissions!" Excited, he races to the job in silhouette, while a not unhappy bum lounges beneath a tree. (see Fig. 25) Our hero is surprised to see a block-length line at the business where he hopes to work. Barks filled this line with a neat array of Duckburg citizenry: fat and tall, smoking pipes and dressed nattily, aged and stooped, and even a pair engaged in fisticuffs. Donald pulls a trick on the supervisor to get to the head of the line and makes his case for employment, which he wins. Pissed at being duped, the head of the sales force is eager to see Donald "get the business," and so he sends our man north, to the Kickmiquik River, to sell "the product." Inspired by their uncle (and,

Fig. 27. The Land of the Totem Poles, 1:3

as usual, joining him on this adventure), the kids run out to get some goods to sell themselves. And with that, we're off.

"Land of the Totem Poles," with its focus on the indigenous tribes of British Columbia, seems to come straight out of the pages of *National Geographic*, and is, at its heart, a comedy of lovely extremes: we go from lazy Duckburg, to the Canadian wilderness, and incredibly this is the British Columbian frontier that is glimpsed in the summer—no snow to speak of. To make matters even more intriguing, when Donald arrives (in a river town called Chilled Foot), he discovers that his product is none other than a truck-sized steam calliope. Undaunted, Donald and the boys rig up a raft, its paddle hooked up to the truck's axle (the calliope sits upon the bed of the vehicle), and sail down the river.

Naturally, there's barely a soul around, until they reach a shack with a sad, long-faced woman who doesn't have the $22,000 to buy a steam calliope. But the boys pounce, selling their wares—cosmetics—to the lady, taking all of her life's savings, $22. Engraged, Donald decides to take the boys' goods to sell himself, leaving them to deal with the calliope.

Their next victim is a hermit living in a cave high above the Kickmiquik, replete with bones laying about the opening. He's barefoot, nothing but a pile of black hair and eyes that suggest he's angry. Donald tries to ply his cosmetics on the man, lipstick and home permanent kits, eyebrow paint "to make your scowl glow in the dark." Nothing doing. Donald's defeated, but as he descends the rocks back to the raft, he tells the boys that the hermit "wants one thing in the world, and he wouldn't say what it is!" Naturally the boys climb up, and naturally the hermit's one desire is… a steam calliope. Ding!

As with this joke, the Ducks reach the end of the line—the Kickmiquik comes to an abrupt terminus in a box canyon, both the end of this particular trail and this particular series of jokes. But Donald sees smoke signals—and now he's going "teepee to teepee" to sell lipstick, on foot. The boys, who need a road or a river on which to haul their machine, are stuck.

The tribe resembles one of the many from the Pacific Northwest, if only for their complex art and well-built wood homes (indeed, Donald will not go "teepee to teepee," as this village relies on wood to fabricate homes.) In a very cinematic panel, Barks' "camera" zooms over a ridge to expose a whole phalanx of people, and we see a gorgeous panorama of a Pacific Northwest Indian village. Staged dramatically on the left, the Chief of the tribe, wearing a ravenshead mask and a long, colorful robe, looks over a bustling scene of people rowing fancy canoes, fishing, and cleaning—all of this ringed by giant totem poles. Little details abound: a woman sleeping beneath the dried fish, rocks on the roofs to keep the slats down, each canoe carved with impressive detail, each fish rendered perfectly on the rack. In a nice touch, one of the tribe is staring at the reader, with a look of irritation, as if we're disturbing this idyllic scene—which, in a sense, we are. This is a moment that is not only gorgeous in terms of art, but it serves as Barks' flexing his research muscles—he clearly spent a great deal of time reading about this village, making sure that it looked as real as possible, exposing his readers to a new culture. Apparently, Barks was reliant on a thesaurus that day as well, as the narration box reads, "In a bosky dell a short distance ahead is the village of the most primitive Indian tribe in North America!" "Bosky"? It means "wooded" or "covered in trees." Well played, Mr. Barks. (see Plate 13)

But the visually gorgeous and accurate panel unfortunately belies the usual 1950s indigenous tropes, as the Indians—again, beautifully rendered as people, not dogs—say things like "Palefaces bad medicine! Sellum Indian bum goods!" The humorous paradox is that the chief of the tribe is ready to reject Donald, claiming that his people are brave, and then, as soon as our man bursts onto the scene, the crowd scatters, even going so far as to try and dig a hole to hide in, such is their terror. Well, as soon as Donald applies lipstick on himself (the horror!) (see Plate 14), the townsfolk come running, overtaking our salesman and using his wares in the worst possible way—drinking cologne, eating soap, putting hair remover on the Chief's noggin. Acting like children, unfortunately.

As with "The Magic Hourglass," "Land of the Totem Poles" is akin to a film from the 1930s or 40s, whose plot and story hum along until they get caught in the mud of racial stereotyping. What's weird here is that Barks clearly read articles whose photographer at least seemed intent on respectfully capturing this culture. That aforementioned splash panel is a more accurate rendering than any Hollywood film up to that point in time (1950) that I can think of, and I imagine it was pretty startling for the white kids of America to come upon.

"Land of the Totem Poles" isn't one of Barks' more profound comics— unlike "Golden Helmet," it descends into slapstick (not bad, but a bit rote in spots), though it does reflect Barks' obsession, through his actor Donald Duck, with rendering perfectly the hard working everyman who seeks to make it big in his chosen profession. Ask yourself: is Donald a failure? Maybe, for although Donald doesn't emerge rich, unlike Willy Loman in *Death of a Salesman*, he's proud, actually flaunting his silly victory at the end of the piece. In the process of saving their uncle, the kids hook up the guts of the calliope to the totem poles, (never mind how it fell apart) and in doing so wowed the Kickmiquik Indians (Barks' joke that further renders the Indians as clowns) with their music. The result? The kids have sold five hundred calliopes to the Indians, paid for by three trainloads of furs. Donald wins the prize as "top salesman," which turns out to be a steam calliope, which the kids have to polish while Donald gloats to Daisy. Set aside the lunacy of selling five hundred calliopes—the product itself is insane. But this giant, steam driven monstrosity serves as a nice parody of nearly all door-to-door products, and the win, and its attendant pride (and punishment), seem to be all that matter to Donald.

As a man who tried, and failed, to attain financial success, Barks made Donald a creature of the daily grind, but, perhaps like Barks (who, in virtually every interview I've seen and read, does not appear the least bit embittered by his various failures or lack of wealth), Donald is a man who loves working, who attains happiness through the process of trying to get things done. As we saw in the pair of stories in which he's a museum guard, Donald emerges from a pair of financial failures feeling as though he's found a spiritual or philosophical success.

Which brings us to the collection of short tales known as the "Brittle Mastery" stories, as they have been referred by various fans and critics. As you'll see, these stories range from 1953—which I personally consider to be the tail end of Barks' best years—to 1963, when he was getting fairly repetitive and his backgrounds lacked the incredible detail of the earlier work, though there's still a lot to like. Basically, the plots of the "Brittle Mastery" series, with one exception, can be summed up in this way: Donald is a "master" of a certain profession: rainmaker, smoke writer, glass repairman, wrecker, and finally, barber. He is not just good at his craft, he is incredible, performing unbelievable feats with precision, with speed, and, in what usually brings him down, with a large degree of arrogance. This arrogance will be his undoing in a typically Barksian way, and often with hilarious results.

The first two stories, "The Master Rainmaker" and "Smoke Writer in the Sky" actually have no titles—these are taken from the Gladstone Publishing reprints. All of these "Brittle Mastery" stories are shorter, and all but "Master Glasser" appeared in the hugely popular *Walt Disney's Comics and Stories* magazines, for a time the best selling comic book in America. Many issues of that magazine featured, in its opening pages, one of these ten-page Donald Duck stories, followed by other Disney comics such as the L'il Bad Wolf, Pluto, Figaro (the cat from the film *Pinocchio*), Mickey Mouse, and others, a bunch of very short, half and two page gags with various characters, plus an actual prose story that was routinely awful. I used to dislike these comics, because they never seemed like a good deal—once as a kid I bought a late 50s Comics and Stories from a comic book shop in Lansing, Michigan, only to be disappointed that the Barks' comic was ten pages and the rest was roughly 35 pages of mediocrity.

But the "Brittle Mastery" stories do not lend themselves to the length of the "novels" (as Barks called them) or "paper movies" (as I'm calling them). They're swift and to the point, building up Donald to ridiculous heights just to bring him crashing down.

Consider "The Master Rainmaker." Barks' opening panel features this narration box: "Sooner or later the science of rain making was bound to be perfected—and the guy that perfected it is none other than Donald Duck, M.R.M. (Master Rain Maker)! The boy is good!" Yes, he is—ridiculously, unbelievably good. Good at his job as Uncle Scrooge is at making money, to the extent that it exceeds disbelief. We open with a farmer requesting that Donald drop exactly two inches of rain on his barley. Not two and a quarter inches, exactly two, onto an "X" shaped field, and not one single drop is to exceed the parameters of that "X." Donald leaps into his crop duster and takes to the skies, where, with a blade attached to the front like a snow plow, he pushes and pulls and prods clouds into that "X" shape, and then seeds it so that it will not give his client one drop too much ("Two inches to the millimeter!" says the farmer, in a funny hybrid of the English and metric units of measurement). From there, Donald is able to drop "slow rain" on a farmer's gooseberries, with a hole cut into the square cloud to keep the wife's drying clothes from getting soaked. And then—bam!—in comes jealousy (in the form of a howling green monster with a pitchfork), when Donald discovers Daisy is having a picnic with his arch-rival Gladstone. Teeth bared, Donald creates a ferocious snowstorm to thwart said picnic, one that not only wrecks his plane, but half of Duckburg as well.

"Smoke Writer in the Sky" is totally bizarre, actually the weakest of the lot, in part because of Carl Barks' seeming disdain for people who hate smog and the fact that Donald actually doesn't seem to be all that masterful. Yes, Donald is an incredible smoke writer, taking, once again, a little plane (visually, the airborne equivalent of his wee car) into the heavens where this time he shapes plumes of smoke into brilliant shapes. Ah, but the rub this time is that Duckburg doesn't appreciate him, as people are complaining about smog (how dare they), and they think the smoke from his plane is contributing to this airborne blight. "Aw, some people would gripe about smoke from a firefly," Dewey complains. My guess is that Barks, who lived in Hemet, a good ninety minutes from Los Angeles, heard folks beginning to complain about LA's considerable smog problem. Perhaps there were requests against making fires, against factories, etc., thus inflaming Barks' mildly right-wing Libertarian "live and let live" philosophy. Today of course it seems like pure lunacy to hear someone bark that people ought to just get used to smog, but there you go.

Donald's work runs afoul of high winds, geese, and the common voter. Turns out that Uncle Scrooge wants to run for mayor (hard to believe), and so hires Donald to make smoke advertisements while he stumps for votes in the city park. After Donald writes "Vote for McDuck" in the sky, and then attempts to shape Scrooge's face in exhaust, it turns out that the old miser mistakenly says that he's "for smog," bringing about the ire of the assembled crowds. The face that Donald makes gets hit by a band of geese, who turn the old duck's mug into a donkey's (the Republican Barks must have intended this political double-entendre of Scrooge being turned into a Democrat) and then, in a series of foul-ups, makes smoke shapes of Scrooge as a shark, a snake, and then an angry bastard chasing a little girl with a broom. Finally, Scrooge shoots rockets at Donald, wrecking the plane, which billows enough exhaust to cloak Duckburg in smog for days. Donald and Scrooge escape to the Isle of Capri and Alaska, respectively, to avoid the wrath of the citizens, who remain behind, eyes ringed with soot, choking in the smog. Like "The Golden Helmet," "Smoke Writer" is filled with negative imagery—when Scrooge stumps for votes, the citizens look worn and weary, and seem to come alive only when Scrooge (the wealthy jerk) is being mocked by his own advertising. Weirdly, Barks' initial criticism, that the anti-smog crowd's going after the wrong man (Donald the smoke writer) is correct: certainly Duckburg's smog problems cannot be placed on the back of smoke writers, which would constitute a very tiny percentage of the junk. Except that, in the end, Barks makes Donald's airplane spew enough exhaust to cloud the city for days, ruining the health of the town.

In "The Master Glasser," Donald Duck is an artisan glass repairman. There is a strange emotional response to Donald's expertise seen here. He is known throughout Duckburg as the greatest glass repairman, and in the first two instances of Donald's coming to the aid of a person, that person is literally crying. The first, a lady has broken her beloved goldfish's bowl. Even the fish is crying (and later, grateful, Barks makes the fish talk—it responds, "chirkle," a word I've not read, seen, or heard before or since). After this repair, he goes to help a man whose headlight on his antique auto has been shattered by a near-sighted woodpecker. The man is weeping. And, again, Donald saves the day.

Problem is, this overenthusiastic response to a pair of minor problems (a fishbowl?) results in Donald's getting a big head (which, as we all know, was metaphorically swollen to begin with.) So when Donald is asked to fix the giant clock on the TV tower, he literally jumps at the chance, knowing his work will now be seen—and appreciated— throughout the city, as the job's going to be broadcast live (for some reason.)

Donald's hubris is incredible, even by his standards. Climbing the clock tower, a new clock face strapped to his back, he faces the TV camera and narrates his own journey. "I am the master glass craftsman of Duckburg! Be sure you remember my name!" (Which he fails to mention). Barks cut away to a family, loafing at home. They're drawn as lazy loafers, another pointed critique of the citizens of his made up town (or perhaps the worthlessness of TV.) They sit, in separate chairs, long faced, bored, and only the mother has a look of any passion—and it's anger. "Do you want to watch this conceited blowhard shatter that old glass?" she barks. "Yes! There's a chance he might slip and fall!" says her weary husband.

Donald removes the old glass with a "super-powered tuning fork" which renders the lens to dust. But Donald's forgetting that he's being broadcast across town: the tuning fork does indeed destroy the old glass (and the new glass as well), but it shatters every television set and glass item within sonic range of the set. Our man is trapped, 300 feet up on the clock tower, while, in a horrifying panel of dark silhouettes raging with clubs, we see Donald, trapped, being closed in on by a lynch mob.

These first three "Brittle Mastery" stories are essentially variations on the theme of self-destruction. Barks could hardly claim that Donald is unlucky, for he's either a slave to his own unchecked anger ("Rain Maker"), incompetent (he is never successful in "Smoke Writer"), or bound by a raging ego that interferes with his intelligence ("Master Glasser".) My two favorite "Brittle Mastery" stories are the next two, "The Master Wrecker" and "Spare That Hair." The first sees Donald as a man of great talent, with a palpable joy in his work, undermined by fate. In the second, he is simply Donald Duck, the world's best God damned barber. And not only does he not fail in this endeavor, he's a badass to boot.

"The Master Wrecker" sees Donald as the King of Wreckers. There is a lovely splash panel showing our man leaping out of bed like a bull, snorting and flexing his muscles. A sledgehammer rests on the wall, and his bed has a little sign that says "Hardrock Bed Co." and has a "mattress" which is really a plank covering stone. His pillow is steel wool, his blanket sack cloth, and his library, toppling over on his desk, is made up of these titles: "The Fall of Rome", "The Crushing of Carthage", "The Toppling of Troy". One of the kids has the first part of his breakfast ready—a cereal of "whole ironwood nuts fortified with zinc, copper, calcium, limestone, brass, and ball bearings!" In the first three panels alone, Donald basically storms around his house snorting. He's ready to wreck things. (see Plate 15)

If there's one theme we can see in these "Brittle Mastery" stories (and absent in the last one, where he's a barber) it's that Donald's expertise is magnified and examined right away. Consider "The Golden Helmet" or "Vacation Time"—like Keaton, Donald is simply a guy eager to go about his business (museum guard, camper), who then rises to great feats, which we're all capable of with the right training and good health. Here, Donald's magnificence is so ridiculously exaggerated there's really no place to go but down.

But "Master Wrecker" sees our man chewed by the maws of fate. He really is a master wrecker, able to make his crane swing a wrecking ball with the grace and dexterity of baseball great Ted Williams. Donald is so effective that, with a tap, he can make the windows of a building gently fall to the ground before he thumps, bumps, and then taps the structure so that it collapses into neat piles of lumber, bricks, pipes, etc., all stacked nicely and ready to cart away.

But this time, after successfully removing a structure thought immovable (a giant concrete fort on the sea—Duckburg sits beside rivers, seas, mountains, on plains... whatever works for Barks), and given a parade, Donald is summoned to wreck yet another building. Gazing at the address—128 Plush Avenue—he sets to work. Problem is, a gnat has landed on the "1," making it appear to be "728 Plush Avenue," the "Top Brass Club," and you can certainly see where this is going. In this, and in the comic I'll conclude with, "No Such Varmint," Donald is thwarted by an insect resulting in a misreading that sets events in motion, a plot point that Terry Gilliam may have borrowed for his film *Brazil*.[1 + 2] There's no point in describing the chaos—it's better if you hunt it down and witness it yourself. But here Donald's proven to be brilliant, and is again, only this time fate has literally thrown a bug into the works, a bug that, I might add, is so mischievous that it remains on the paper and then, when Donald realizes his mistake, flies off while saying "Hee hee!" Now, this could be proof of Donald's horrible luck (it is), but again, Barks wasn't content to just rub our hero's nose in it—Donald escapes to the Little America research base in Antarctica, where he destroys igloos to great applause... from penguins. Even better, his nephews look on with pride, and Donald bows, smiling like a Buddha, before his audience.

"Spare That Hair" and "No Such Varmint" (the latter a full length Donald Duck comic) are two moments in which Barks gives us his star as a humble working man, one a barber who only wants his dough, and the second a simple-minded man who knows exactly what he wants in life, to the chagrin of his nephews. "Hair" is short and simple, as neatly conceived as the finest short comedies of Laurel and Hardy,

.................

1   *In Brazil*, a fly disrupts paperwork which causes the wrong man to be arrested, tortured and executed, wrecking the lives of various people and almost undermining the government.

2   The Ducks have certainly influenced a ton of other people's work, if you go by this great piece in *Cracked* online, which suggests they helped make *Inception*, *Raiders of the Lost Ark*, and Manga—check it out here: http://www.cracked.com/article_19021_5-amazing-things-invented-by-donald-duck-seriously.html.

with Donald in full command of his little barber shop, able to take on all comers. You're a professor with a massive ball of hair that covers all your features? Donald will make it square, which is perfect, since everyone calls you a square anyway. An orchestra conductor whose hair fell out in an attack of fever, and need a bouffant to command the respect of your musicians? You've come to the right place. Problem is, a circus has come to town, a gorilla escapes, who makes a beeline for Donald's shop. Using all the wiles in his considerable arsenal, Donald manages to give the brute (whom he thinks is a circus roustabout), a shave and a haircut, making the monster appear feeble, not a raging ape necessary to entertain the crowds. Furious, the circus ringmaster goes ape himself, and tries to throttle the barber, to no avail. "Just a feather-pickin' minute, bud!" Donald shouts, just before he turns the tables, "Don't try to collect anything from a barber! Especially when you owe him three bucks!" In this case, Barks seemed to be suggesting that Donald, for once, is a proud member of a larger group. He's not saying "don't try and collect anything from me," but rather, "a barber." Donald's inclusion seems to protect him from fate (ape accidentally wandering into his shop) or even ego. For once, Donald is a success, albeit a modest one, who simply worked hard and wanted to be paid for his labors... much like the man who drew him.

We'll close with what might be Barks' most Zen-like story, a beautiful tale that fills me with an almost inexplicable sense of comfort and joy. No Such Varmint was released in the spring of 1951. Barks was in the midst of that horrendous marriage to an alcoholic, one so chaotic that he often retreated to a hotel room to avoid having his work torn to pieces (or himself chopped with a meat cleaver.) His stories from that time vary from The Magic Hourglass' cynicism to "Vacation Time's" optimism. Like the latter, Varmint was perhaps a balm for the artist's troubled mind. In this story, the nephews serve as the catalyst, but an oddly negative one: they're embarrassed for their uncle, and shove him into an adventure that he doesn't seek.

The splash panel that opens "No Such Varmint" again reveals Barks' joy in drawing seascapes. A ship, "laden with gold from the Alaskan mines of Scrooge McDuck," sinks after hitting "a mysterious object." The panel is striking: the sinking ship's stern rises dramatically in the air, smoke billowing parallel to its angled deck. It sinks to the bottom of the water, in an inlet with rocky shores and pine trees (later it's called Barnacle Bay.) The next panel assures us not to worry, as the crew rows away, utterly calm, the captain standing at the bow, scratching his head. "Now, what do you suppose caused that?" he asks, perplexed but not as alarmed as you'd think someone would be who had just survived a shipwreck. Tonally, this was Barks signaling to us that this would be a more relaxed adventure. If they're not going to worry, why should we?

In two panels, Barks had set the tone—in panel three, he begian to lay the groundwork of the story. Our three nephews loaf in a beautiful park—and compare the next few panels depicting Duckburg with the Burbank of "Maharajah Donald." The city is now vivid, with its palm trees and lakes, the perfect place for citizens to relax. "Some people are great people," Huey muses, "and some are bums!" There can be no doubt who they're talking about, and no doubt whether he's great or a bum. From there we get a roll call of so-called "great" people: Flinthide, a banker; Shyster, a lawyer (a good one, famous for his "wit and oratory"... I guess Barks had not wrestled with divorce lawyers yet); Groanbalm, the doctor; Markup, the merchant, the writer Scribble, and Tryle N. Error, not the chemist, but "the mighty chemist!" All of these men, a veritable cavalcade of the city's finest, are meant to serve as a shocking contrast to our hero, ambling down the same path, singing "Oh, the world owes me a livin'—" while the boys hang their heads in shame.

But Donald is different now. In the other work stories, our actor shows his confidence, only to be undermined by any number of internal or external forces. In others, he's a normal guy who is pushed to excellence. Here, however, Donald has the sublime confidence of a person who has, perhaps, achieved satori, the Zen term for being able to see clearly one's own nature. Donald will not hear of the boys' dismay that he is not pursuing the world's riches, for he has a profession at which he is great: he is a snake charmer. And a great one.

The boys are ashamed, but Donald, unruffled by the kids' obvious displeasure, begins charming all over the park, luring the happy creatures out of hiding with his music. Donald and his beasts are creatures of pure joy—the snakes are apple-cheeked, Donald at one with nature as they dance in a circle.

Undaunted, the nephews read of a man who measures people's heads to determine their lot in life, and decide that their uncle has to figure out his real profession. Reluctantly agreeing to this quackery, Donald sits in the chair while the doctor studies his cranium. Once again, fate appears in the guise of a bug. Donald's reading of "115" becomes "11.5" when a "tired bug" lands on the monitor. According to the doctor's fat guidebook, 11.5 means that Donald is going to be… a great detective.

But Donald doesn't want to be a great detective. Once again, he retreats to the serenity of the park and begins playing his music with the accompaniments of satisfied snakes. But the boys remain convinced in science's superiority (albeit ridiculous pseudo-science) and set up a "Detecktif" agency, place an ad, and wait for someone to hire their uncle. Their first client is none other than Scrooge McDuck, who needs to get some answers as to what sank his ship.

Off they go to Barnacle Bay. In a gorgeous splash panel we see the whole of the bay, with a volcanic lake in the distance. Like a great director, Barks had made each panel fraught with significance—the boys look outward, toward an invisible quarry that their uncle is supposed to be investigating; Donald, on the other hand, is looking backwards, away from the action, and to the woods, where he hopes to entertain the region's snakes.

What we soon discover is that the boys are the detectives, and Donald is happy entertaining the music-starved serpents of the forest.

It is the nephews who survey all the equipment Scrooge has sent them, the boys who push Donald onto the glass-bottomed boat, and the boys who uncover many of the clues, like the gouged sea bottom where the ship once lay. Which begs the question: what would the boys' brain waves have revealed? We don't know if 11.5 vs. 115 is a measurement of intelligence (the higher the number, the smarter the bean?), or just a number on a scale. Earlier, when the doctor consults his guides, he scrolls down toward 11.5 and reads "Fiend... chicken thief... human fly..." suggesting that that number does not sit in the best company. And yet, detective doesn't seem like the dopiest job in the world. Perhaps the nephews should have had their skulls scanned as well.

Out on Barnacle Bay, the boys are disgusted as Donald rejects their pleas to actually get on with the work of detecting—but the disgust is mutual, as this is work that Donald clearly did not agree to perform. "Don't bother me with small troubles! I'm dreaming up a new tune!" Spoken like a true artist. Forced out in the middle of the water, he tries out a "special number for charming big snakes," and man, does he get one. Here's the "Varmint" of the title—the goofiest, friendliest sea monster ever to emerge out of the drink.

Donald's terrified, and in this case, maybe rightfully so. He's a coward—as any of us would be—in the face of a 500 yard snake rising out of the water. Escaping to the shore, the boys are convinced that they've solved this little mystery (they have), that they've got to figure out where this creature's hidden the boat which contains all the gold. Donald, for his part, is content to play in such a way as to arouse worms to rise from logs (for a "bright future" selling bait), and then dreams of training snakes for vaudeville (a fun little reference of Barks'—vaudeville was long dead by then, so was he a fan?) or creating a "rattlesnake band." As he practices (and dreams) by the crater lake, his music captures the attention of the giant beast, who rises, wearing a mask of almost pure euphoria. Donald tries to run away, but the eponymous varmint grabs him, and only releases Donald when he begins to play. In a delightful series of panels, the snake can be seen cavorting in the water, while Donald, exhausted, plays on.

Through the machinations of the boys, Donald is freed, the snake slithers away, having had barrels of black pepper tossed in its mouth. As it retreats, it hauls Scrooge's ship into the depths with it, thus removing any evidence whatsoever of the ship or its very presence. Donald, exhausted, wants nothing more to do with snake charming, and the boys have failed at their (Donald's) detective work. All have failed. Or have they?

In the end, we return to the park, where the fat cats of Duckburg saunter by, proud and stately in their accomplishments. The boys repeat the lines that I think sum up our man quite perfectly: "People are funny!" Dewey says, gaping into space as though he's just revealed a profound truth. "Some are great..."—and we cut to Donald, now picking up trash in the park and seeming to almost dance with joy in doing so—"...and some are like Unca Donald!"

Very few, indeed. With Donald Duck, Barks examined the nature of work in America like no other comic book artist, examined the nature of citizen heroism, of the joy in adventure and learning (such as the expedition in "Lost in the Andes") for its own sake. Donald's losses are tremendous—most of the stories here show him not achieving his goals—but they do reveal a character who understood that not taking risk is far worse than taking the risk, and the failures in living this life are actually triumphs. We usually think that for everyone who has succeeded—the Scrooges of the world—there are failures. But there are not just people who fail—like Donald—but, sadly, there are people who never tried. Donald's failures, then, reveal a profound and spiritual success. Failing to try, failing to live, seemed, to Barks, like the worst fate of all.

# BIBLIOGRAPHY:

Ault, Donald, ed., *Carl Barks: Conversations*, 2003, University Press of Mississippi.

Andrae, Thomas, *Carl Barks and the Disney Comic Book: Unmasking the Myth of Modernity*, 2006, University Press of Mississippi.

Dorfman, Ariel and Mattelart, Armand, *How to Read Donald Duck: Imperialist Ideology in the Disney Comic Book*, 1991, International General, New York.

Websites
http://www.cbarks.dk/
http://www.thecarlbarksfanclub.com/
http://inducks.org/
http://www.michaelbarrier.com/
http://home.earthlink.net/~vathek/index.html (Geoffrey Blum)
Carl Barks interview http://www.youtube.com/watch?v=8rmIXv5i1TA (Thanks Mike Haeg)
Five amazing things invented by Donald Duck:
   http://www.cracked.com/article_19021_5-amazing-things-invented-by-donald-duck-seriously.html

The comics came from these sources. They do appear in other sources, but these are the ones I own and used for research:

Maharajah Donald
*Donald Duck*, New York: Abbeville Press, 1978,
    and
*The Carl Barks Library of Walt Disney's Donald Duck Adventures in Color*, No. 6, Prescott, Arizona: Gladstone, The Bruce Hamilton Company

Lost in the Andes
*Donald Duck*, New York: Abbeville Press, 1978,
    and
*The Carl Barks Library of Walt Disney's Donald Duck Adventures in Color*, No. 10, Prescott, Arizona: Gladstone Publishing, The Bruce Hamilton Company
    and,
Barks, Carl, *Walt Disney's Donald Duck: Lost in the Andes*, Seattle: Fantagraphics Books, 2011

Luck of the North
*Donald Duck*, New York: Abbeville Press, 1978,
    and
*The Carl Barks Library of Walt Disney's Donald Duck Adventures in Color*, No. 12, Prescott, Arizona: Gladstone Publishing, The Bruce Hamilton Company

The Gilded Man
*Donald Duck*, New York: Abbeville Press, 1978,
    and
*The Carl Barks Library of Walt Disney's Donald Duck Adventures in Color*, No. 20, Prescott, Arizona: Gladstone Publishing, The Bruce

Hamilton Company
and,
Barks, Carl, *Walt Disney's Donald Duck: A Christmas for Shacktown*,
Seattle: Fantagraphics Books, 2012

## The Magic Hourglass
*Donald Duck*, New York: Abbeville Press, 1978,

## Vacation Time
*The Carl Barks Library of Walt Disney's Donald Duck Adventures in
Color*, No. 18, Prescott, Arizona: Gladstone Publishing, The Bruce
Hamilton Company

## The Golden Helmet
*Donald Duck*, New York: Abbeville Press, 1978,
and
*The Carl Barks Library of Walt Disney's Donald Duck Adventures in
Color*, No. 20, Prescott, Arizona: Gladstone Publishing, The Bruce
Hamilton Company
and,
Barks, Carl, *Walt Disney's Donald Duck: A Christmas for Shacktown*,
Seattle: Fantagraphics Books, 2012

## Land of the Totem Poles
*Donald Duck*, New York: Abbeville Press, 1978,
and
*The Carl Barks Library of Walt Disney's Donald Duck Adventures in
Color*, No. 13, Prescott, Arizona: Gladstone Publishing, The Bruce
Hamilton Company

## No Such Varmint
*The Carl Barks Library of Walt Disney's Donald Duck Adventures in

*Color*, No. 17, Prescott, Arizona: Gladstone Publishing, The Bruce Hamilton Company

## The Master Rainmaker
*The Carl Barks Library of Walt Disney's Comics and Stories in Color*, No. 24, Prescott, Arizona: Gladstone Publishing, The Bruce Hamilton Company

## Smoke Writer in the Sky
*The Carl Barks Library of Walt Disney's Comics and Stories in Color*, No. 31, Prescott, Arizona: Gladstone Publishing, The Bruce Hamilton Company

## The Master Glasser
*The Carl Barks Library of Walt Disney's Donald Duck Adventures in Color*, No. 24, Prescott, Arizona: Gladstone Publishing, The Bruce Hamilton Company

## Master Wrecker
*The Carl Barks Library of Walt Disney's Comics and Stories in Color*, No. 45, Prescott, Arizona: Gladstone Publishing, The Bruce Hamilton Company

## Spare That Hair
*The Carl Barks Library of Walt Disney's Comics and Stories in Color*, No. 47, Prescott, Arizona: Gladstone Publishing, The Bruce Hamilton Company

## PETER SCHILLING JR.

Peter Schilling Jr. is the author of *The End of Baseball*, and *Mark Twain's Mississippi River*. He also writes about film and the arts for a variety of publications. He has been reading and studying Carl Barks' entire catalogue since he was a child.

Plate 1. Maharajah Donald, 11:5-7

Plate 2. Lost in the Andes, 17:5

Plate 3. Luck of the North, 19:1-2

Plate 4. Luck of the North, 22:3